MW01480881

MARRIAGE SOS

30 Lifelines to Rescue Your Relationship in One Month

Debra Macleod, B.A., LL.B.

© Debra Macleod 2014

All rights reserved. No part of this publication may be reproduced, stored in a retrieval system, or transmitted in any form or by any means, electronic, mechanical, photocopying, recording or otherwise, without the prior written permission of the author.

Debra Macleod asserts the moral right to be identified as the author of this work. www.MarriageSOS.com

The author is not engaged in rendering professional advice or services to the individual reader. The relationship strategies presented herein are for general informational purposes and are based on the principles of effective communication, conflict resolution and positive interactions within marriage: they may not be suitable for all or serious marital problems. The author is not a mental health practitioner and this book is not appropriate in situations of mental illness or instability, or physical, sexual or emotional abuse of a spouse or child. Only the reader can judge the suitability of this book's content to his /her specific situation. The author will not be held liable for any act or omission allegedly arising, directly or indirectly, from the use or misuse of this book.

Cover photo: Heart Lifebuoy. © corund. Provided by Shutterstock.com
Inside Illustration: doodle lifebuoy © Netkoff. Provided by Shutterstock.com

Contents

PART I

A Crash Course in Marriage

Divorce: Behind the Scenes

Although I have for years been in the business of saving marriages and helping couples keep their families together, I took a somewhat backward route to this career path. How so? Well, I actually began my career as a divorce mediator. I was in the business of dissolving marriages and families.

The time I spent as a divorce mediator gave me an invaluable and unique perspective that too few people and marriage professionals have.

It gave me a birds-eye view of what causes a marriage to fail. In a way, I guess I am now something of a relationship "reverse engineer."

I know what causes the end product – that is, divorce – to happen, and I use that knowledge and insight to help couples avoid divorce and achieve a much better end product – a happy marriage.

When I worked as a divorce mediator, I saw how my clients had run their relationships into the ground. How they talked to each other with contempt, criticism and self-centeredness.

How they stopped showing each other affection, appreciation and adoration. How they let themselves go, let sex slip off the radar, let resentment fill their hearts, let their kids call the shots, let someone else in their bed, let it all slip away.

And how they were now sitting in my office, pretending to be interested in the art on the walls, while really they were scared out of their wits that they were going to lose custody of their kids, ownership of their home, half the assets they had spent years toiling for, the respect of family and friends and a lifestyle they used to love.

It's an interesting position to find oneself in: Sitting in a room with two people who used to be madly in love, who used to laugh at the same things and ride roller-coasters together, who used to share their bodies in pleasure, who cried when their first child was born and snuck into the living room in the middle of the night to put presents under the Christmas tree – and who now can't even stand to look at each other.

Sometimes, the anger, resentment and even hatred between them are palpable. That's almost guaranteed if there's been an infidelity...or two...or three.

At other times, the room is packed with wall-to-wall sadness, regret and fear. The air is heavy with the things they still want to say to each other. Fools.

There were things I wanted to say to them, too. Not to all of them. Some of them needed to call it quits. Whether it was abuse, chronic cheating, true incompatibility or just a streak of belligerent narcissism, they were putting themselves – and more importantly their kids – through hell.

But some of them didn't really need to be there. Some didn't really want to be there. Some of them even looked a little shocked by the whole thing: *How did it get this far?*

Some of them tapped their fingers on the table or cast their soon-to-be ex-partner sideways glances, as though they were waiting for him or her to say something. Something…soft? Hopeful?

Those were the ones I wanted to grab by the collar, shake and scream, "You prideful idiot! Do you know what your problem is? You have no humility. You have no staying power, no sense of loyalty to the person you committed your life to or the kids you brought into this world!"

I would envision myself gripping their collars more tightly. "What do you think your life is going to look like when you're eighty years old, huh? Who's going to visit you? If you couldn't make this marriage work, what makes you think the next one will work? You've broken up your family, and for what? So you can drag your kids into a blended family with a step-parent, and then make the same mistakes in that marriage so they can go through another divorce? When are you ever going to get your act together?"

Deep breath. That is what I envisioned myself saying – even as I read it, I hate how self-righteous it sounds. And yet no matter how much humility I muster, I can't escape the feeling that I'm right about a lot of it.

When it comes to marriage and divorce, many people are short-sighted. They're impulsive. When the passion starts to cool off and real life – work, money problems, familiarity – starts to heat up, they point to the person closest to them, their spouse, and blame it all on him or her.

They start to say that they're just "not compatible" or that they're "growing apart."

Instead of working together to reignite the passion and resolve their specific problems, they submit to their growing feelings of resentment and hopelessness.

They start snapping at each other and begin basting in their own unhappiness, much of which is self-inflicted. They stop talking or having sex.

Before they know it, their hard feelings and snarky comments escalate to the point that one of them throws up their arms and says, "That's it! I want a divorce!"

And that's when I would come in. Fun job, hey?

Some divorces come out of so-called "starter marriages," ones that last only a few years and usually involve people in their very early twenties.

Some of these people put more thought into their iPhone contract than they did their marriage contract, so you'll forgive me if I say their break-up wasn't a real shocker.

These breakups were still sad, though, especially in those situations where the couple managed to pump out a few kids during their scrappy three-year marriage.

These are children who will never remember their mom and dad living under the same roof, and who will never know the happiness and well-being of having constant access to both biological parents.

These are parents that will spend years having to shuffle their shared biological kids between their respective houses, fighting about who gets who for Christmas or birthdays, and often worrying themselves sick about their co-parent's weird new boyfriend or girlfriend and how that person is treating their children when alone with them, behind closed doors.

Yet the divorces that really rattled me were the ones that happened after decades of marriage.

I couldn't fathom how a couple could spend twenty or thirty or more years of their lives – their entire youth and middle age – being married to the same person, raising a family, and then – poof! – no more.

To me, that's a depressing thought.

Wouldn't all those years seem like wasted time? How could one look back on all those Christmas mornings and summer vacations and not feel like all those experiences were fake? Wouldn't you feel like you had to cut out a portion of your life and forget about it altogether?

A spouse is that constant presence in our lives that records our life's experiences. We play those experiences back together, as husband and wife, especially when times are quiet.

When the kids leave home. When we're snuggled in bed. When one of our parent's dies. We talk about our shared life experiences and they come to life again, like an old projector shining images of birthday celebrations on the wall.

We talk about the times we've had and we re-live them together, full of pride and gratitude for the life we've managed to pull off together.

But if you don't have that life-long person beside you, who's been recording all of that? With whom will you play back your happiest times when the sun begins to set on your days? If you've had kids, they'll be grown and busy with lives of their own.

What will you do when you hear a song that reminds you of that long-ago road trip you took through Death Valley, the one where you stood under the starry night sky and then jumped back into the car when something scurried over your foot in the darkness? You can't exactly just dial up your ex-spouse and say, "Wasn't that an amazing night?"

What do you do with those photo albums that are packed with pictures of birthdays, school concerts, dogs and decades and seasons of your life? Wouldn't it be strange to look back at them from the distance of many years, and see the arms of your ex-spouse around your waist?

Wouldn't all of those experiences seem somehow hollow? Wouldn't some part of you start to think back and – if you were honest with yourself – wish you could have a do-over?

That's what I mean by people being short-sighted. I have enough professional experience with divorce to know that it doesn't always fix a person's problems the way he or she thinks it will.

Sometimes, it just creates a new set of circumstances and problems. It makes your life messier, more complicated and gives you more baggage.

Sometimes, it leads to regret and second-thoughts. "Should I have tried harder? Might we still be together?"

Nowadays, people love to slam marriage. They love to talk about how it's just a piece of paper or how it doesn't improve your chances of staying in love with your partner.

I recently did a television segment that discussed how the "honeymoon phase" in a marriage wears off after two years and how spouses tend to become less happy after that point. According to some people, this was a reason to avoid marriage.

Yet the marriage nay-sayers are missing an important fact. This so-called honeymoon phase – where it's all hormones and butterflies – tends to wear off in *any* romantic relationship around the two-year point.

Whether you're married, living together or just dating, after about two years you're going to experience a similar change in the intensity of your partnership.

That leaves you with a decision to make about the lifestyle you want to lead.

If you want, you can change partners every now and then so that you can re-experience the honeymoon phase. As soon as it starts to wear off – which it will – you can break-up and look for someone new again. Most of us know someone who lives like this. They go through relationships like we go through razors. When one gets dull, you just dispose of it and replace it with a new one.

Your other option is to commit to another person for life. You can make the choice to transition with maturity, gratitude and grace to the various phases that your marriages will go through over the years.

You can learn to value and appreciate the things that a long-term marriage has to offer: security, loving friendship, children and family life. And if things do get a little dull now and then, you sharpen it up instead of throwing it away.

Many of the people who slam marriage are, not surprisingly, divorced. Considering the years I spent in the divorce business, I should probably feel as cynical as they do about marriage.

But I don't. In fact, I feel quite the opposite. I'm a hopeless romantic and always will be.

There is no substitute for a happy marriage. It is one of the most reliable paths to find meaning, companionship and joy in life, and it provides the safest, most secure environment in which to raise kids who have a sense of belonging and well-being.

It's the ideal we all strive for, and it is within our grasp.

Marriage SOS: Rescuing Relationships

I was a few years into my practice as a divorce mediator when something weird and unexpected started happening in my office.

More and more, couples who had booked appointments for divorce mediation were starting to reconnect right before my eyes. As our sessions proceeded, their voice tones and expressions softened. Their body language opened up. They started making eye contact and talking to each other, rather than just talking through me.

For many of my clients, the conversations that I mediated between them in my office were the first time they had communicated effectively in years. Although my initial goal was simply to make them get along for the sake of their kids, my unique approach to couples' mediation began to spark long-forgotten feelings of friendship and love between them.

This was an emotional process for many couples, especially as they began to realize how poorly they had treated each other and how little they had understood each other.

Before I knew it, new clients were phoning me up and – instead of asking for divorce mediation – were asking whether I could help them save their marriages.

Word of mouth had spread that I was offering a no-nonsense and "counselling-free" way for couples to reconnect and resolve their problems. And that was something many people wanted.

Eventually, I went with the flow and changed the focus of my private practice from divorce mediation to couples' reconciliatory mediation. That is, I began to help couples avoid divorce, save and improve their marriages, and keep their families together.

I particularly began to see individuals and couples whose marriages were at a crisis point. Indeed, it was this urgent "rescue" approach that inspired me to call my practice Marriage SOS. The majority of my clients came to me as a last-ditch effort to save their marriages. They wanted fast results.

People who are in unhappy marriages are usually not motivated enough to attend ongoing professional marriage help – if you can't help them see a glimmer of hope in that first hour or so, they're done.

That's why many of my clients were counselling drop-outs. They had attended traditional – that is, psychology-based – marriage counselling or talk therapy; however, that process was just way too slow and theoretical. Clients seemed unable to make any real-world headway for months, if any headway could be made at all.

At first, that annoyed the hell out of me. I'd think, "So, you've spent years running your marriage into the ground and treating each other like shit, but you expect me to fix it in an hour?" After a while, however, I just accepted it. Frankly, that's just the nature of the business I'm in.

In fact, I now think that all married couples should have a similar sense of urgency when problems, even small ones, arise. It's far better to tackle issues right away than to ignore them and let them simmer for years until they finally boil over and make a mess that no one can clean up.

That's why I wrote this book – because I know that couples who are having marriage problems need to dive in, fast, to rescue their relationship. *Marriage SOS* offers a condensed inventory of the thirty most effective, straightforward and fast-acting strategies – I call them lifelines – that I use in my practice to help couples target and tackle their issues as quickly as possible.

Whether you are working through these marriage-saving strategies as an individual spouse or as a couple, their purpose is to spark positive change in your marriage from the very first day that you start to use them.

With each passing day, your and your partner's motivation to save your relationship increases, and your marriage gets stronger.

The strategies I've included in this book are as practical and fast-acting as they come. They are based on the principles of effective communication, conflict resolution and mediation; however, I have put my own spin on them over the years to make them relevant to marriage and immediately usable to couples in crisis.

The goal of these strategies is to improve understanding, encourage more positive interactions, move past specific problems or crisis situations, and enhance intimacy and marital devotion.

Most importantly, they are designed to do this as quickly and simply as possible while always balancing the perspectives and needs of both spouses.

You will never save your marriage if you're not willing to see things from your partner's point of view as well as your own.

Indeed, many of the strategies in this book encourage you to take the first step. By changing your behavior for the better, you inject positive change into your marriage. In so doing, you are likely to spark a positive reaction from your spouse, who in turn will be motivated to do his or her part.

This approach has an infinitely better chance of success than blaming your partner for everything and demanding that he or she change first. Good luck with that.

Marriage SOS also includes "crisis care" to help couples survive such marriage emergencies as affairs and broken trust, money problems, blended family issues and coping with a belligerent, defensive or critical spouse. Rather than going into great depth for each issue, this content is designed to help you get your head around these complex issues in a preliminary, general way.

This material complements the thirty lifelines and is used in conjunction with them so that spouses can gain essential insight into their problems while at the same time taking steps to remedy them.

Unlike psychology-based counselling or couples' therapy, my approach assumes that there are no mental health issues in the marriage.

In my opinion, most marriage problems are not mental health issues. Many stem from poor communication, misunderstandings, negative interactions, bad habits and an inability to move past specific issues (i.e. broken trust, loss of intimacy, lack of appreciation or support, divided loyalties, etc.) in a realistic way. Indeed, I believe that applying a bandage unnecessarily soaked in psychology can make some marriage problems worse.

That being said, if you feel that you or your partner have mental health issues, or if there are any safety issues or indicators of abuse in your home, you need to consult the appropriate resource immediately – the police and/or a lawyer, and a mental health practitioner.

In terms of both its content and approach, *Marriage SOS* offers you a no-nonsense and realistic way to save your marriage. I've spoken to countless clients over the years who have told me that they purchased marriage self-help books; however, these books rarely save or even improve marriages.

Don't get me wrong – some of these books have excellent advice and couples would be wise to take it to heart. The reason most marriage self-help books don't work is because they are too long, too academic, too complicated, too full of fluff and filler.

Most marriage self-help books contain pages upon pages of largely unnecessary anecdotes about the counselor's past clients or theories, and offer exercises that are far too complex, abstract and time-consuming for troubled couples to actually work through or put to use in their life.

Very few of my female clients ever said they finished one of these marriage self-help books, and I don't recall a male client who ever claimed to finish or find value in one.

After hearing this kind of frustrating feedback for years, I knew precisely the kind of marriage-saving book that I needed to write. It had to be a book that even the most emotional, broken-hearted, hopeless, angry or impatient spouse would be able to find value in.

It had to be a book that didn't waste time, but rather bulls-eyed the most common reasons that marriages fail and provided easy but effective marriage-saving strategies. Moreover, these strategies couldn't be theoretical. They had to be concrete "do this, don't do that" directions.

I also knew these strategies had to come with a timeline. Many couples who are languishing in unhappy marriages are not willing to devote endless months of their lives to see whether their marriage can be saved. They want to get on with their lives. They either want to see proof that the marriage has hope or they want to move on and file for divorce.

That is the main reason I chose thirty as the magic number of strategies I would include in *Marriage SOS* – one new strategy a day over the course of one month.

In my professional experience, I have found that most couples who are having marriage problems are willing to devote one month to see whether the relationship can be saved.

When it stretches on longer than that – and especially when little or no progress is being made – people tend to give up. It may not be right, but it is what happens.

I have had many clients who have come to me saying, "We're done." Yet when I ask them whether they are willing to try a few new things for a short one-month period, they are usually game to do so.

At best, they will see and feel positive changes in their marriage and they will begin to reconnect. At worst, they will move toward separation in a more amicable way. For couples who have children, either outcome is preferable to a bitter divorce and the years of nasty, petty interactions that are destined to follow.

So whether you're "done" or just slowly drifting apart, whether you're trudging your way through problems that never seem to end or you're in the middle of a marriage crisis, give *Marriage SOS* one month of your life to see if your relationship can be saved.

The insight and strategies in *Marriage SOS* that I will ask you to incorporate into your relationship are things that every marriage needs not just to survive, but to thrive.

It isn't enough to stay married. Couples must stay happily married. Even if you feel your marriage is relatively strong, this book can prevent it from weakening or growing apathetic, loveless or passionless.

As the old saying goes, an ounce of prevention is worth a pound of cure. Nowhere is that more true than in married life.

The daily marriage-saving strategies in Part III of *Marriage SOS* serve as lifelines for couples who find themselves in all manner of relationship distress and who need something to cling to, something to guide them to a better, safer place amid a storm of emotions and uncertainties.

Perhaps they have tried other approaches and nothing has worked. Perhaps they need simple, straightforward directions to see whether they can arrive at a sunnier shore.

Before you begin the 30-day journey to a happier marriage in Part III, however, let's take a crash course in marriage and divorce here in Part I.

That is, what is marriage and what does it have to offer in today's world? Generally speaking, what tears it apart and what keeps it together?

After that, we'll do some crisis care in Part II by looking at some initial ways to survive marriage emergencies from just-discovered affairs to blended-family battles and everything in between.

Doing this kind of prep work will give you the best chance of success as you begin your month-long endeavor to rescue your relationship.

The State of Matrimony

The institution of marriage is, in anthropological circles, known as a cultural universal. That is, it is common to all human cultures on the planet and is a fundamental component of the human condition.

It reaches back into the dawn of the human experience. It is also subject to change. Many of the changes that marriage and by extension family life have undergone since antiquity, at least in our Western culture, have happened alongside the rise of women's and children's rights, and have overwhelmingly been for the better.

Yet when we stand back and take an objective look at the state of marriage in our modern society, it sometimes seems that this fundamental component of the human condition is gasping for breath.

Why? Well, the explanations are different depending on who you ask.

A marriage therapist will have one explanation, while a jilted wife or husband will have another. A married right-wing male conservative politician will have his opinions, just as a divorced liberal feminist will have hers.

These various opinions will be a blend of professional and personal experience, values and perspective.

Professionally and personally, I have a strong bias toward marriage. I think a happy, healthy marriage is one of the most fulfilling relationships a person can have on this Earth.

People who are happily married tend to be healthier, less stressed and live longer. And at the end of their lives, they are able to look back with pride and passion at the lifelong, intimate friendship they shared with their husband or wife, a life full of history and memories.

To me at least, that brings far more meaning to one's life than a string of past partners and broken homes.

I also think a good marriage fosters the best and most stable environment in which to raise children who, having been led by example, know what it takes to keep a marriage and family together and are therefore more likely to enjoy those blessings in their lives than are children of divorce or family breakdown.

Children who grow up in a happy home expect to live in a happy home as adults. That's important, since it is our expectations than often determine our destiny in life.

I've spent many years working in-the-trenches as a couples' mediator. During this time, I've helped many couples resolve all manner of conflict and improve communication, interactions and intimacy.

On a professional level, I've realized that good interpersonal skills and appealing personality traits are the nuts and bolts of any long term relationship, including the one we have with our spouse.

Yet I'm also a wife and a mother and I know there's more to the equation. On a personal level, I've gone through the emotional ups and downs of married life and I can relate to people who are going through them.

For this reason, *Marriage SOS* doesn't just focus on relationship skills or strategies. It also brings an emotional dimension to the decision you made when you chose this book – the decision to see whether you can save your marriage.

Why Do Couples Get Divorced?

There is no single or easy answer to the question of why marriages end in divorce.

Yet in my professional and personal experience, I have definitely seen certain traits, behaviors and qualities that tend to put marriages on the line and lead to life of misery, if not divorce court.

I've outlined a number of these on the following pages.

- Broken trust. While some couples can recover from infidelity, an emotional or physical affair changes the marriage forever. It may be forgiven, but it is never forgotten. Even many years after an affair, the betrayed partner will find his or her mind racing to an unpleasant place when his or her spouse is late for dinner, doesn't answer the phone and so on.

- Divided loyalties. When one spouse feels his or her partner's loyalty is to another person, whether a family member or friend (especially an opposite-sex friend), a sense of resentment and betrayal is bound to arise.

Sometimes divided loyalties are inappropriate, as when a husband prioritizes his mother over his wife. At other times, they are a necessary fact of life, as when a divorced man and father starts a new family. He will (or at least should have) responsibilities to his previous children.

- Finances. Money troubles such as debt, secret purchases or disagreement on how to allocate resources can cause much conflict in a marriage. Money problems can spill over to cause problems in all areas of a couple's life, from parenting to sexual intimacy and everything in between. They are a leading source of stress and anxiety as well.

- **Unpleasant personality types.** People who are self-focused, narcissistic know-it-alls or who have "hair triggers" that quickly have them escalating into infantile fits of indignation or belligerent temper tantrums are the most difficult – and unappealing – of partners. Sometimes, the person is just an immature or egocentric individual who has an inflated sense of himself or herself.

At other times, however, high-conflict personality types actually have a personality or mental disorder that needs to be treated by a mental health practitioner.

It is impossible to have a happy, healthy marriage with an individual who will not get these behaviors under control or receive treatment, particularly as these behaviors are associated with domestic abuse. They also make life a living hell for any children who are unfortunate enough to live in the home.

- **Lack of appreciation.** Spouses who feel that their efforts or sacrifices are not acknowledged or appreciated tend to be unhappily married. In fact, not feeling appreciated is a top complaint of divorcing couples.

- **Assumptions.** Jumping to unfounded, negative assumptions is one of the most common pitfalls in communication. When a spouse makes a nasty assumption about a partner's words, behaviors or motives, it becomes incredibly difficult for that partner to explain his or her true intentions or feelings.

- **Cheerlessness.** Couples who communicate with flat, negative or nasty voice tones, and who interact with each other with indifference or emotional apathy, create a cheerless vibe in their marriage.

- **Laziness.** Spouses who "let themselves go" physically, or who stop doing "the little things" to make their partner feel adored, let laziness get the better of them.

- **Child-centered marriage.** We all love our kids. But marriages that exclusively revolve around the kids' lives, activities and preferences run a real risk of losing the romantic element that is so central to the marriage bond. They also demonstrate a poor marriage role-model to kids.

- **Skewed priorities.** Whether it's working overtime, doing endless favors for friends or in-laws, or disappearing every weekend to partake in a hobby or sport, some spouses begin to prioritize other people and activities over their partner and marriage.

- **Little or no empathy.** Some spouses are either unable or unwilling to see or feel things from their partner's point of view. They often come off as uncaring, immature and self-righteous, and are usually long on criticism and short on humility.

- **Lack of marriage manners.** From walking across a clean floor with their boots on to texting a friend during what was supposed to be a romantic dinner-for-two, some spouses seem to forget the most basic of courtesies when they are in their partner's company.

- **Loss of intimacy.** Reduced sexual enjoyment and frequency can cause a serious disconnect between spouses and result in a loss of physical intimacy. At the same time, a decrease in non-sexual gestures and words of affection – embracing, kissing, cuddling, pillow talk – can lead to a loss of emotional intimacy.

- **Lack of spiritual connection.** Many couples – even those with otherwise functional marriages – feel that their marriage is lacking a spiritual dimension, one that would bring greater meaning or comfort to the life they share.

This is sometimes true with non-religious or secular-minded couples who reject the religious doctrine or supernatural elements of certain belief systems; however, it is also often true of couples who come from a religious background that, as life goes on, they feel is increasingly irrelevant or antithetical to married life.

Marital & Family Disconnect

If you lived through the 1980's, you might remember the iconic tee-shirt that said, "Kill Your Television!"

Today, it would read, "Kill Your Wi-Fi!"

Nowadays, I rarely have an appointment with a client where the issue of technology doesn't arise in one capacity or another. And it's never in a positive way.

The pervasive and invasive quality of modern technology has had profoundly negative effects on the solidary and happiness of modern marriages and families.

Of course, I'm not talking about electricity and the type of technical advances that make modern life comfortable and livable.

I'm talking about gadgets.

Toys. Smartphones. Tablets. Laptops. Social media sites. Internet surfing. As we connect to these "personal" forms of technology, we disconnect from our spouses and families.

For example, take the issue of infidelity. In days gone by, it was trickier to start an illicit affair.

First off, how did you know whether the object of your extra-marital affection was attracted to you and game to cheat with you?

Well, you'd have to tread carefully and throw out a few salacious hints. It took guts and time, and there was the risk of face-to-face rejection or, even worse, the dreaded, "How dare you! I'm going to tell your wife/husband!"

Today, that initial hurdle is now solved.

All you need to do is sign up for an online dating site, many of which are designed specifically to facilitate extramarital affairs between "like-minded" people.

Or, if you prefer someone more familiar, you can always look up an ex-partner or old flame on social media.

You can "confide" in each other and talk about your marital troubles until your relationship turns sexual, which you both knew from the start was going to happen.

And what about the challenge of communicating with your forbidden paramour? In days gone by, you might have to call him or her at home and risk an angry spouse answering the phone with a vicious, "Who the hell is this?"

Or if you weren't brave enough to call his or her house, you would have to wait until you were away from your respective homes. If you trusted your co-workers to keep it quiet, you might be able to talk at work. If not, you'd have to wait and meet up after work – and then explain to your spouse why you were late.

Now, the communication hurdle is also solved.

Cheating spouses can sit at their own supper tables, only an arm's length away from their unsuspecting partners and smiling kids, all the while "sexting" under the table with their lover via smartphone.

By the time dinner is over, the cheater and his or her partner in crime have had their kicks.

And what if a suspicious spouse asks, "Who are you texting?" Well, that's easily solved. You just accuse him or her of being "jealous" or "controlling," insist that the conversation is "private," and then change your password so he or she cannot read your guilty messages.

It almost couldn't be easier.

Indeed, many affairs begin today because of ease of opportunity and the way that texting between opposite-sex friends or associates can very quickly lead to a false sense of intimacy.

In the past, the desire to stray might come and go before a spouse had the opportunity to act on it. Many bullets were dodged that way. Now, once the idea arises, the opportunity is everywhere. By the time the thrill wears off and the regret sets in, the damage is done.

While extramarital affairs are the cruelest and most destructive handiwork of modern technology, not all problems caused by our gadgets are so inherently sinister.

Some tech-related marriage problems are just incidental by-products of using various forms of personal technology, even in an innocent way. That doesn't make them any less irritating, though.

When you stare at a gadget instead of looking into your partner's eyes, or you post an update to social media instead of living in the moment with your spouse, you send an unintentionally hurtful message: "This gadget is more interesting than you. I'd rather spend my time with it than with you."

Ouch.

The technology issue is even more problematic when it comes to parent-child interactions. We as parents often complain that our kids, especially as they get into the pre-teen and teen years, spend too much time playing video games and staring at computer screens. This can cause a disconnect in the family unit, too.

Yet I can't say I'm blameless when it comes to the obsessive use of technology. More than once I've heard my son say an exasperated, "Mom! Did you even hear what I said? You're just staring at your phone!" Yep, I'm guilty, too. Guilty of doing what I tell others not to do, and then feeling guilty about it afterward.

Now, I make a conscious effort to lay my phone screen-down or close the lid on my laptop when I'm talking to my son. I do the same thing when my husband talks to me.

As a bonus kickback, I've noticed that they've started showing me the same respect and attention. I guess the whole "lead by example" thing really does work.

What Makes a Model Marriage?

Suffice it to say, the quality of the marriage between a husband and a wife, especially if and when they become parents, sets the tone for the household. Some homes are full of friendship, love and laughter. You can feel it the moment you walk through the door.

Other homes are filled with anger, negativity and an almost toxic dislike between those who live there. You can feel that, too. As spouses, we model a way of married and family life for our kids. That's why it's so important to have a model marriage.

Couples must have a passionate spirit about their marriage. They must have a burning desire, through all the ups and downs of married life, to keep the promises of fidelity, friendship, love and devotion that they made to each other.

Too many people waste away their years, energy and emotions in marriages that lack the luster of happiness and passion. By so doing, they squander their own lives. If they have children, they model a pitiful example of marriage that can reduce their kids' chances of enjoying the many benefits that a happy marriage has to offer.

When I give marriage advice, I call upon my experience as a divorce and couples' mediator. That is, I look at the behaviors, attitudes and habits that tend to accompany relationship breakdown – such as those outlined in the previous two headings – and then I encourage couples to do the exact opposite. It makes sense. And it works.

To have a model marriage, a couple must have good marriage habits. I've outlined a number of these here.

● Trust. This seems obvious, right? But to be clear, I'm not just talking about trust as a general concept or emotion. I am talking about trust in terms of behavior.

It is an age-old adage, and a true one, that a person who has nothing to hide hides nothing. Trust is achieved and maintained by transparency. Spouses should know each other's passwords for computers, social media sites, email accounts, smartphones, etc.

Opposite-sex friendships – including texting or spending time with opposite-sex friends, especially those a spouse does not approve of – should be kept to a bare minimum. There are exceptions, but that's the general rule.

In fact, maintaining such friendships is often incompatible with the notion of marriage itself. Spouses should be open in respect to where they're going and with whom, and should be let their partners know if they will be late and why.

- **Loyalty.** Again, this isn't just a vague concept or emotion. The marriage and one's spouse must come first.

Part of the marriage vow is to be loyal to your spouse above all others, including your own parents, siblings and friends. (A clear exception is when a partner has obligations – moral, financial, time-wise and emotional – to previous children.)

In addition, spouses must behave in a way that says to their partner, "I have your back." If a friend or family member has a conflict with a person's spouse, that person must rise to their spouse's defense. This is especially so if the conflict is a public one. Even if the spouse is in the wrong, a person must stand by him or her in public.

Behind closed doors, you can call them on their behavior. But when in the company of others, you must always have each other's back.

- **Good money management.** Both spouses must be equally aware of and responsible for finances – the good and the bad – and be on the same page in terms of spending, saving, investing and so. They must also agree on the big picture in terms of property and retirement, so that they can realistically plan for their future.

- **Have a pleasant personality.** Humility, patience, good humor, open-mindedness and an easygoing, forgiving nature are the types of personality traits that every spouse should strive to have. The quality of a marriage is only as good as the quality of each spouse's character.

- **Be appreciative.** Each and every day, a spouse should acknowledge his or her partner's contributions and sacrifices, whether they involve working, parenting, house-cleaning and so on. Words and gestures of appreciation are essential to a person's sense of worth.

- **Don't make nasty assumptions.** If your partner says or does something that is out of character or that you don't immediately understand, cut him or her some slack until you get more information. Assume the best about your partner.

- **Cheerfulness.** This doesn't mean you have to float around your house in a constant state of glassy-eyed bliss. It does mean, however, that your relationship should be characterized by a general spirit of good cheer that involves friendly, respectful voice tones as well as happy, loving interactions.

  Smile when your partner enters the room. Wink when he or she walks by. If your partner is in a bad mood, challenge yourself to do or say something to cheer him or her up. Make sure that your home has a vibe of happy togetherness to it.

- **Keep it up.** Spouses often take care of themselves and behave better in the early phases of a relationship than they do when they've been married for years. Don't let things like good health and surprise gestures (flowers, favorite suppers, weekend getaways) fall off the radar. Don't take your partner for granted or assume that you're set for life because you're married. Stay motivated to be an appealing partner to your spouse.

- **Put your spouse ahead of your children.** Don't get me wrong – if the house is on fire or you only have one granola bar during the food shortage of a zombie apocalypse, of course you must put your kids ahead of your spouse or yourself.

Your kids are the first people you pull out of a burning building and the first you feed when stomachs are empty; however, you don't need to make such life or death choices every day, do you?

Remember that you and your spouse are the sun that your kids revolve around, not the other way around. In time, they will have their own marriages and families.

By modeling a loving marriage and functional family life, you set them up for success. Let them see what it looks like when a man and woman are in love. Let them thrive in the knowledge that your marriage, and by extension their home life, is rock solid.

- **Get your priorities straight.** We're all busy. We're all pulled in different directions – work, spouse, friends, chores, free time and so on. Yet it is essential to prioritize one's marriage above all.

This doesn't mean that we have to spend all of our time with our spouse. Indeed, between work and other obligations, it can be difficult to find couple time; however, quality is more important than quantity. Even if you're short on time, there are ways to make your spouse feel as though your marriage is your top priority in life.

- **Be empathetic.** Happy spouses have the desire and the ability to both see and feel things from their partner's perspective. When in conflict with their spouse, they focus on understanding their partner's feelings and point of view instead of merely rising up in defensiveness to prove that they are "right."

When their partner is going through a hard time, they try to identify and be a shoulder to lean on, rather than passing judgment or dishing out self-righteous advice.

• **Mind your manners.** Are you remembering to compliment your spouse on his or her new haircut? Are you remembering to say please and thank you?

After years of marriage, it is common to withhold from our beloved the kind of common courtesies that we extend to acquaintances and strangers without a second thought.

• **Anticipate.** Happy couples have a knack of being able to anticipate what their partner's needs or preferences will be, or what kind of mood he or she will be in following certain events.

This ability to anticipate comes from a combination of familiarity and empathy, as well as an authentic desire to meet – or preferably exceed – their partner's needs.

• **Faithfulness.** Sexual and emotional fidelity is a fundamental part of marriage between two people. But there is another kind of faithfulness: a faithfulness to the institution of marriage. Many marriages have their rough spots and temptations; however, devoted spouses commit themselves not just to their partner, but to their marriage.

Even when spouses don't feel an abundance of love or desire for each other, they must have an unwavering commitment to the marriage contract. Instead of breaking that contract (or their vows), they must make a conscious effort to reignite feelings of love and desire. These are perhaps the most successful of all marriages.

Remember the words of Germaine Greer:

"A successful marriage requires falling in love many times, always with the same person."

- **Maintain intimacy.** Emotional intimacy can be generally understood as intimacy that doesn't directly involve sex, but that makes two people feel connected.

Words and gestures of affection, pillow talk, cuddling, embracing, flirting and flattering, are all behaviors that enhance emotional intimacy, which is an integral part of marriage.

Emotional intimacy also means behaving in ways that strengthen the overall partnership, from sharing chores to getting on the same page about spending and parenting.

Physical intimacy is also integral to marriage. It involves sex that satisfies both partners in terms of frequency, variety and mutual pleasure.

Couples who realize that emotional and physical intimacy are two sides of the same coin, and who prioritize and value each equally, increase their odds of having a lasting marriage.

- **Nourish a spiritual bond.** Even couples who do everything right in their marriages and who consider themselves loving, devoted spouses may find greater meaning and comfort in their relationship by bringing a spiritual dimension to their marriage.

A marriage without conflicts
is almost as inconceivable
as a nation without crises.

- Andre Maurois, French writer

PART II

Crisis Care

Marriage SOS is a marriage-saving guide that is designed to prevent and remedy a wide variety of relationship problems, especially those that are generally associated with relationship breakdown and divorce.

It does this by providing general but essential insight into what makes a marriage successful (or unsuccessful, as the case may be) and particularly by providing simple strategies that individual spouses or couples can try over a month-long period to see whether their relationship can be rescued.

Yet some issues are so common and complex that they warrant more attention and consideration, even in a general-scope manual of this nature.

These issues are: broken trust and infidelity; money problems; sex and intimacy; parenting; in-laws and ex-partners; blended families and step-children, and; dealing with a belligerent, critical or defensive spouse.

We'll take a longer look at each of these issues in this part. Again, keep in mind that this book's purpose is to present you with general information and encourage a pro-marriage attitude. If you are facing serious or long-standing issues, you may need to supplement with information that is more specific to your struggle.

Even if your marriage problems don't seem to conveniently fit into one of these categories, it is still worth your while to read through the material in this apart.

Relationship troubles are often diffuse and multifaceted, and you and your spouse may have different ideas about what your issues really are.

It is common for one partner to say "Our problems are about money," while the other partner says, "I don't trust my spouse." Read everything. You never know when a piece of advice or insight will hit home.

Broken Trust & Infidelity

Of all the emergency situations or urgent problems that arise in a marriage, none cause the degree of emotional shock or require the level of crisis care that infidelity does.

It's a gut-wrenching experience to discover that a spouse has been unfaithful. It's equally devastating to hear a spouse confess to infidelity, even if the confession was given as a sincere attempt to save the marriage.

Living in suspicion – *Is my spouse having an affair?* – can be just as bad. Unfortunately, many spouses who suspect their partner of cheating are correct.

Classic signs include spending more time at work, financial spending that cannot be accounted for, sudden self-improvement efforts (i.e. joining a gym, dressing better), secretive and defensive behavior and even an increased sexual interest in the other spouse. There are usually red flags.

Today, a common red flag is the flashing message light on a smartphone, and a spouse who ducks into a different room to read it or respond to it.

"Innocent" texting between opposite-sex friends can quickly escalate into a sexual dialogue due to the false sense of intimacy this medium provides.

People start sharing private details of their lives, swapping exaggerated sob stories about how miserable their marriages are and, before you know it, they think they've made a meaningful connection with someone they barely know.

In the worst cases, some people even think they've "fallen in love" with their texting or extramarital paramour.

When their conscience or better judgment kicks in, they ignore it and instead rationalize the behavior by saying they've found their "soul-mate," that they were never truly happy in their marriage or – at the pinnacle of self-delusion – their children will respect them more if they "follow their heart" to find happiness, even if it means breaking up the family.

Until a cheating spouse gives their head a shake and comes to their senses, their spouse and kids will continue to suffer for their self-indulgent behavior.

Of course, some marriages have serious problems and some people may be drawn to another person who seems to provide what their spouse cannot or will not.

Yet adding a "third wheel" to your marriage – the Other Woman or the Other Man – will only add to your problems while preventing you from putting your focus and energy where they can do the most good.

The truth is that most people (and their children) will be happier if they can bring what is missing from the marriage back into it, thus keeping their family together.

If you are a wayward spouse who is wondering whether you're in love with an extra marital bedmate, take a look at the following key questions.

The more you answer "No," the more likely it is that your affair is driven by temporary, hormonal lust and not genuine, lasting love.

- Have you performed mundane duties with this person (i.e. yardwork, shopping, home repairs, financial planning, co-parenting, getting insurance quotes, etc.)?

- Have you spent time with, or money, on this person's parents, siblings, family and close friends?

- If you suddenly became bankrupt, would this person stand by you and do whatever it took to financially recover (i.e. live in a basement suite and take a dishwashing job to support you)?

- Have you seen this person at his or her worst (i.e. sick, emotional, stressed, etc.)?

- Would you be proud to introduce this person to your children, parents, family and friends? Would you be proud to share the details of this person's past, and how your relationship began?

- If this person died or became incapacitated today, would you be willing to raise his or her children and settle his or her outstanding debts?

- If you died or became incapacitated today, would you give this person Power of Attorney over your finances, property, minor children and personal health decisions? Would you trust this person to manage your children's trust fund or care for your aging parents?

- If you were to leave your underage children in this person's care right now, are you just as confident that he or she would take as many measures to protect your children from harm (i.e. not leaving them in the car unattended, watching them in a crowd) as your current spouse would?

- If you could never have sex with this person, would you still put as much effort into seeing her or him?

The above questions may sound plodding, but that's the point. Love puts down roots and is rational. Lust is a faster ride. It's a roller coaster that people hop onto for the thrill of it.

The sudden loops give you butterflies but, without love to keep you on the rails, the ride always ends abruptly and usually with nothing to show for it but a sickening feeling in the pit of your stomach.

In a new and healthy relationship, lust is the force that draws two people together and motivates them to stay together so that their romance has time to mature and transition to genuine feelings of love.

If you do it right, you lust after your partner until you fall in love with him or her.

And then you keep working at it – reigniting those feelings of lust now and then – so that you can feel the warmth of both lust and love for the rest of your lives.

Let's say that a spouse realizes he or she has simply fallen into lust, not love, and decides to end the affair. How does one do this?

Ending an affair has to be done quickly, permanently and often with "proof" that one can show a doubtful spouse, such as a text or email. The marital interloper's contact information must then be deleted and blocked from phones and computers.

In some unfortunate cases, a cheating spouse may be hesitant to tell his or her extramarital bedmate that the affair is over. The spouse may feel guilty or fearful about ending it, or may not want to give up "the rush" of having someone lust after them.

This type of inaction, flip-flopping or reluctance is misplaced loyalty in the extreme.

It can do irreparable harm to the marriage as the betrayed spouse sees his or her partner as even more unfaithful, uncommitted and unreliable. Even if the betrayed spouse "sticks it out" until the wayward spouse steps up and ends the affair clearly and decisively, that betrayed spouse may in the future exhibit deep resentment for how long it took his or her partner to re-commit to the marriage.

In my experience, it is impossible to move past infidelity and rebuild a marriage while a spouse is involved with another person. The wayward spouse's energy and affection are too divided, and the betrayed spouse cannot live in such an emotional state of uncertainty and powerlessness without harboring deeply negative feelings.

Remember that the marital interloper does not require, and is not entitled to, significant time or effort when it comes to ending the affair.

He or she should not have had a presence in the first place, and the sooner he or she gets the boot, the better.

There is no need for private meetings to "find closure." An unfaithful spouse who claims differently is adding to the insult and injury he or she has already caused the other spouse.

Spouses who make excuses or refuse to cut contact with the interloper are not sincere about saving their marriages.

Full accountability on the part of the unfaithful spouse is also essential if the marriage is to survive. There may be legitimate marital problems that contributed to the affair; however, most people have marriage problems at one time or another, yet not all people break their vows.

If you've cheated, you're at fault. Refusing to admit the infidelity – even in the presence of clear evidence to the contrary – or shifting blame onto your spouse will likely be the last nail in your marriage's coffin. Practice honesty and humility.

The wayward spouse should also keep two more important things in mind.

First, be patient. Don't become short or irritated by your spouse's questions, sadness or anger, or tell him or her to "Get over it already!" A betrayed spouse will experience many flashback emotions, even after he or she has appeared to put the infidelity behind him or her. Be patient. Be patient. Be patient.

Second, do not downplay the betrayal. Even if it was an emotional affair, do not say, "We didn't sleep together, so it doesn't matter." Instead, always **fully acknowledge the impact your behavior has had on your spouse** and the toll it has taken on his or her mental, emotional and even physical well-being.

Let's move on to assume the unfaithful spouse has done all the right things: he or she has ended the affair, cut ties with the other person, and has been fully accountable for his or her actions.

He or she has been patient with his or her spouse, and has consistently acknowledged – with love and humility – the impact the betrayal has had on the spouse and perhaps even their family life.

At this point, he or she is likely to face some tough questions from a heartbroken spouse. Who was she/he? How many times did you do it? How did you do it? Where? How long did it last? Was she/he more attractive than me? Do you fantasize about her/him?

The answers to some of these gut-wrenching questions may be more valuable than the answers to others.

For example, a spouse is fully entitled to know the identity of the extramarital girlfriend or boyfriend, whether there was sexual activity (and whether it was protected or unprotected), where they usually met and how long the affair lasted. Moving past infidelity is practically impossible without these kinds of answers.

Other questions that a betrayed spouse might ask – although perfectly understandable and natural to ask – may be less helpful.

What did you do in bed? What positions were you in? How many orgasms did you have? How did you touch him or her? How big was his penis? How large were her breasts? Did you do things we haven't done?

These are the gory details.

If you're a betrayed spouse who is agonizing over how many details you want or need, you may wish to ask yourself the below questions and use them as general guidelines.

How much information do I require from my spouse to reassure me that he or she:

a) has ended the affair
b) loves me and only me, and
c) will work to save our marriage?

Be realistic but honest with yourself about the information you need. Once you hear a gory detail, you can't unhear it.

It may be helpful to write down your questions and sit on them for a few days.

Even if you don't change your mind about needing to know the gory details, at least you will have had time to collect yourself before asking them.

People often say that their marriage ended because their spouse had an affair; however, infidelity isn't always the cause of marital breakdown. Often, it's a symptom of a relationship that is already unhealthy.

If a person isn't getting what they need from the marriage, they may go outside the marriage to have their needs met. This doesn't excuse infidelity. There's no excuse for it.

But there may be an **explanation** that can help couples understand why it happened. That's important, since they can't rebuild their relationship until they know why it fell apart.

Having an explanation can also help both partners, especially the betrayed spouse, focus on purposeful thoughts instead of just languishing in heartache, confusion and a sense of powerlessness.

Trying to figure out why a spouse cheated can be a confusing, emotional process. There are three questions that – although simple and broad – can help bring some initial focus and structure to the process. You need to start somewhere, right?

Question #1:
What complaints has my partner expressed about our marriage?

People often say their partner's affair "came out of nowhere." Yet when they are ready to really think about it, they will often admit that there were problems. When questioned, they can usually recall a spouse's past complaints.

A wife might say, "He complained that we weren't having as much sex and were always bickering," while a husband might say, "She complained that I never listened to her or spent time with her."

This question isn't meant to suggest that the betrayed spouse is to blame for the affair or that his or her complaints are less important. It is meant to help a betrayed spouse begin to discover why his or her partner turned outside the marriage.

Question #2:

Was this an emotional affair, a physical affair or both?

It's a stereotype that men have physical affairs while women have emotional affairs. Both genders have both types of affairs. And both can be very difficult to get past. An emotional affair can be especially difficult to overcome if the cheating spouse feels that he or she is in love with the other person.

A physical affair can be difficult to overcome if the betrayed spouse feels sexually inadequate or cannot get the sexually explicit "visual" out of his or her mind.

Nonetheless, the distinction between an emotional and physical affair is important to make, as it may lend insight into what was missing from the marriage.

Question #3:

What was so appealing to my spouse about that situation?

In many cases, a cheating spouse isn't drawn to a specific person. The affair may have had little to do with physical attraction, true love or natural compatibility.

Rather, it may have had more to do with how the Other Man or Other Woman made the spouse feel about herself or himself.

This is a critical distinction to make, since it can "depersonalize" the affair to some extent, thus allowing both spouses to understand it more clearly.

By depersonalizing the affair partner, the focus is brought back onto the marriage, and the Other Man or Other Woman becomes powerless and inconsequential. The Other Man or Other Woman could have been anyone. They were nothing special.

After a couple has some insight into why their relationship fell victim to infidelity, they can take those first steps toward rebuilding trust. This involves two important things: transparency and repeated positive experiences.

First, transparency.

A partner who has broken a spouse's trust should be willing to account for their whereabouts at all times. They should be willing to share passwords to their computer and online accounts, and to leave their smartphone unlocked and in view of their spouse.

Moreover, they must be willing to do this with empathy and patience, without growing indignant or saying, "Get over it! How long are you going to watch my every move?" Keep in mind that you've broken your spouse's trust and therefore given him or her reason to doubt you.

At the same time, a betrayed spouse must have the self-assuredness to insist on a reasonable degree of transparency, one that allows them to function and feel at ease as they work on repairing the marriage.

Some cheating spouses will try to shift the focus onto the behavior of the betrayed spouse by saying, "You're controlling!" or "You're obsessed by this." Others will pout. Still others will become belligerent or insist on their "privacy" after only a week or two of transparency.

Unfaithful spouses who act in these ways, or who try to make the betrayed partner feel controlling or paranoid, are not sincere about saving their marriages.

The second requirement for rebuilding trust is repeated positive experiences.

Infidelity is one of the most negative experiences a person can undergo in their lifetime. A couple trying to rebuild a relationship must therefore counteract a flood of bad feelings with an even bigger flood of good feelings.

Kind words, affectionate voice tone, loving interactions and displays of appreciation, commitment and friendship are needed to remind a couple that their marriage is worth saving.

Working through the thirty strategies in Part III is an easy and effective way to ensure that positive experiences keep happening in your marriage over a month-long period.

Money Problems

There are few other issues that can have such pervasive negative effects on a marriage as money problems. Have you ever seen the game Whack-a-Mole? That's how money problems affect a marriage. They continuously pop up in any and all areas of your life and, no matter how hard or fast you try to hit them, they keep popping up, here and there, again and again.

Money problems stand in the way of true partnership in marriage. They can compromise a person's health, sense of well-being and security, and curtail their quality of life. They can cause partners to turn on each other with accusations and resentment, and can lead to profound feelings of stress, hopelessness and frustration.

Money problems impact intimacy, reducing sexual frequency and enjoyment. They chip away at married and family life, causing untold anxiety in the home – anxiety that, too often, children feel the brunt of.

Money problems can kill your marriage and buy you a divorce as fast as any other marriage emergency. There's no such thing as "it's only money."

Money is power. Some people use it for good, others for evil. It's no different in marriage. If one spouse makes considerably more money than the other, or if one is the sole breadwinner, it sometimes happens that money comes to represent power in the relationship. This unfortunate situation can undermine the very essence of partnership in marriage.

A cliché but common scenario involves a husband who is the sole provider and a wife who is a stay-at-home mom. While this arrangement can work beautifully for many couples, in some situations the breadwinning husband may use money as a way to control his wife, or to make her feel that she is not equal to him.

He might say something like, "I make the money, so I decide how it's spent," or "I work all day, what do you do? How much do you contribute?"

This often leads to a dysfunctional relationship where "what's mine is mine, what's yours is yours," where – of course – the breadwinning spouse claims ownership and control of much more. This is the opposite of a partnership.

When we think of a spouse who "controls the money," we might picture him or her holding the purse-strings and dispensing money to a partner like a parent dispensing an allowance to a child.

But a partner who spends freely – too freely – is exerting a problematic type of control too, especially if he or she continues to misspend despite knowing the toll it is taking on their partner's sense of financial security and well-being. This type of behavior can also undermine the essence of partnership in marriage.

"His and Her" money is another common situation that works for some couples but not for others. It may be that both spouses work, but keep separate bank accounts. They may say, "We'll use my money to pay the mortgage and your money for all the bills."

Yet even if the bills are split evenly, one spouse – whether because he or she makes a higher income or saves money better – will be left with more in the bank.

Nevertheless, this arrangement does work for some couples. It may even be advisable or necessary in some situations, especially with couples who have been previously married/divorce and have children from prior relationships that they need to care for.

Some people insist on separate bank accounts as a way to maintain independence and privacy.

While this works fine if both spouses feel that way, it can be problematic if one spouse prefers a joint account and pooling of resources.

He or she may interpret the other spouse's separate account as an "escape clause" or as insurance for a quick way out of the marriage. This can make a spouse feel insecure and resentful. A spouse might say, "So you trust me enough to have children with me, but not enough to share your money?"

These scenarios offer a quick peek into how money matters can turn into control issues, as well as challenge a person's core values, sense of partnership and ideals about marriage.

For couples who are struggling with money problems, the discussion about this issue – including any decisions about money management – should therefore always begin with a discussion about the nature of partnership.

The purpose of a discussion about partnership is not to moralize or persuade your partner that your ideals about partnership and money management are superior.

The purpose is to gain insight into each other's feelings, behaviors and assumptions.

Spouses who have this insight into each other are more cooperative, respectful and effective at solving problems on a practical level (i.e. budgeting, setting up accounts, financial planning) than those who lack such insight.

Many of the strategies in Part III will facilitate a good discussion about money and partnership. At the very least, you should read the lifelines in Day 5 (get to the root of arguments) and Day 28 (learn to communicate) before having this kind of conversation.

Keep in mind also that our emotions affect our spending habits and purchases. That's a fact that advertisers rely on, isn't it? *Buy our aftershave and this beautiful woman will sleep with you! Use our lipstick and this gorgeous man will fall in love with you!*

My dad once told me, "Never go car shopping when you're in a good mood." Why not? Because when we're happy, our thinking tends to be less critical. We are more likely to buy a car based on its joyful, shiny red paint rather than on less thrilling factors such as fuel mileage, reliability and safety.

But the opposite also holds true. An unhappy person may use "retail therapy" as a way to self-soothe. A man who has just discovered his wife's affair might purchase that shiny red sports car to feel better.

A woman who feels unattractive to her spouse might go on a spending spree to boost her self-perception. Parents, realizing they haven't been spending enough time with their kids lately, might spontaneously buy them a costly and high-maintenance pet. Emotions (whether good or bad) and finances can be a problematic mix.

It's a simple formula. Misspending + Overspending = Debt. And excessive debt leads to stress, poor health, resentment and serious marriage problems.

To make matters worse, misspending spouses are often clueless about their true financial situation. Not only can this cause profound resentment and anxiety in the other partner, it sets a family up for disaster.

If the financially aware spouse becomes incapacitated or there is some type of emergency, the financially unaware spouse is unable to manage the household finances. Again, this is the opposite of partnership.

Some overspending spouses say, "My partner is a saver, but I'm a spender. We have to enjoy life in the present, not worry about the future."

While that's certainly true to some extent, this sentiment is often used as an excuse for a misspending spouse to continue to get his or her way, and to avoid financial responsibility.

This sentiment also disregards the other partner's opinion and makes it much more difficult for him or her to enjoy the present.

It some cases, a penny-pinching spouse would like to relax and spend more in the "here and now," but is afraid to do so because he or she fears the other spouse will see that as a ticket to spend more freely.

But it isn't always one spouse who misspends. Often, both spouses are guilty of poor money management. The good news is, such a situation is the easiest to improve, since there is no finger-pointing or blame. Both spouses recognize their own bad habits and can work as a team to break them.

After a couple has achieved greater insight into what is causing the money problems and is able to discuss this issue as true partners, it absolutely essential that they take real-world steps to remedy their situation. Financial planning on a practical basis must happen.

Without actual follow-through in terms of budgeting, spouses will continue to let money chip away at their marriage. Unfortunately, this "action phase" is where many couples drop the ball. All talk and no follow-through can increase a spouse's feelings of fear, resentment and hopelessness.

To avoid such a setback, you and your spouse should take three steps together:

a) Agree on a common financial goal for your future
b) Assess your current financial situation, and
c) Create a balanced, realistic budget

These are outlined in the pages that follow, and can help couples get started as they take these first steps toward financial success; however, it may be necessary to consult a financial specialist in situations where finances are not straightforward, such as business ownership, financial responsibilities to previous children, or where debt load has become unmanageable.

At the very least, the following pages can give you a framework within which to discuss your goals, get a general idea of your current financial reality, and begin to conceive a budget that takes into account your expenses and forces you to evaluate your spending habits. If you are fighting about money, this should be done on an "emergency" basis.

a) Agree on a common financial goal for your future

This may include goals to pay off a mortgage or debt, as well as goals about vacationing, retirement, paying for a child's post-secondary education, etc.

_____

_____

_____

_____

_____

_____

_____

b) Assess your current financial situation

This may include income (salary, tips, bonuses, pensions, etc.) and deductions (tax, pension plans, union dues, etc.).

INCOME

_____ $_____

_____ $_____

_____ $_____

_____ $_____

DEDUCTIONS

_____ $_____

_____ $_____

_____ $_____

_____ $_____

Net Monthly Income

(income minus deductions) $_____

c) Create a realistic budget

The budget framework and monthly expenses presented under this heading are for example purposes only. They are not exhaustive and may not be applicable to your particular situation. Nonetheless, I wanted to include a basic budget framework in this book so that couples could begin to get the "big picture" of their finances.

Most importantly, I hope the inclusion of this budget framework will motivate couples to work together to tackle this serious issue without delay. The sooner a couple feels like they are moving forward, the sooner they start to feel better about things.

In addition to using this budget framework, couples who are trying to solve their money problems may find helpful direction by reading the lifeline in Day 30 (resolving conflict) in Part III.

A fool and his money are soon parted. I would pay anyone a lot of money to explain that to me.

- Homer Simpson, *The Simpsons Television Show*

HOUSING

Mortgage / Rent	$_____	Taxes	$_____
Insurance	$_____	Electricity	$_____
Heat	$_____	Water	$_____
Telephone	$_____	Cell Phone	$_____
Internet	$_____	Cable TV	$_____
Home Repair	$_____	Lawn Care	$_____
Other	$_____	Other	$_____

HOUSING SUBTOTAL $_____

FOOD & HOUSEHOLD

Groceries	$_____	Lunches	$_____
Dining Out	$_____	Cleaners	$_____
Toiletries	$_____	Laundry	$_____
Hair Care	$_____	Pets	$_____
Other	$_____	Other	$_____
Other	$_____	Other	$_____

FOOD & HOUSEHOLD

SUBTOTAL $_____

CHILDCARE

Nanny $_____   Daycare $_____

Babysitter $_____   Other $_____

CHILDCARE SUBTOTAL $_____

CLOTHING

Children $_____   Self $_____

Spouse $_____   Other $_____

CLOTHING SUBTOTAL $_____

TRANSPORTATION

Car Loan(s) $_____   Insurance $_____

Registration $_____   Fuel / Oil $_____

Maintenance $_____   Parking $_____

Bus / Taxi $_____   Other $_____

TRANSPORTATION SUBTOTAL $_____

HEALTH & MEDICAL

Health Fees	$_____	Insurance	$_____
Dental	$_____	Eye Care	$_____
Prescriptions	$_____	Massage	$_____
Counselling	$_____	Diet Needs	$_____
Other	$_____	Other	$_____

HEALTH & MEDICAL

SUBTOTAL $_____

EDUCATION

School Fees	$_____	Books	$_____
Supplies	$_____	Activities	$_____
Other	$_____	Other	$_____

EDUCATION

SUBTOTAL $_____

RECREATION

Kids' Sports	$_____		Lessons	$_____
Books	$_____		Movies	$_____
Travel	$_____		Club Fees	$_____
Gifts	$_____		Alcohol	$_____
Other	$_____		Other	$_____
Other	$_____		Other	$_____

RECREATION SUBTOTAL $_____

MISCELLANEOUS

Donations	$_____		Savings	$_____
Life Insurance	$_____		Other Tax	$_____
Other	$_____		Other	$_____

MISCELLANEOUSS

SUBTOTAL $_____

TOTAL OVERALL EXPENSES $_____

TOTAL OVERALL INCOME $_____

OVERALL SURPLUS / SHORTFALL $_____

Notes:

_____

_____

_____

_____

_____

_____

_____

Sex & Intimacy

Couples experience all manner of sexual and intimacy issues: this section will address some of the most common problems.

Let's start with different levels of sexual drive or interest between partners, a situation that creeps into millions of marital bedrooms. The spouse with the higher drive may feel neglected, rejected or unloved, and may react in a number of ways. He or she may withdraw into silent resentment, self-consciousness or sadness.

Alternatively, he or she may whine or complain about the lack of sex. Worse, he or she may criticize the other partner or threaten to "get it somewhere else." At the same time, the spouse with the lower drive may feel resentful or pressured, or that he or she is simply being "used" for sex by the other spouse.

Don't let different sex drives
drive your marriage into the ground...

For some couples, so-called "maintenance sex" can bridge the distance between two different levels of sexual drive. It involves the spouse with the lower sex drive engaging in sexual activity to satisfy the spouse with the higher sex drive. The partner with the lower drive may participate in sexual intercourse or may simply pleasure the other partner, whether with his or her hands/mouth/body or with a sex toy or erotic aide to add variety.

For many couples, maintenance sex isn't just about sex. It is about staying close and meeting each other's needs; however, it must **only** be used in marriages where both spouses agree that it will be requested and performed with loving respect and affection, and with a frequency that is acceptable to the spouse with the lower sex drive.

The partner with the higher drive may still have to self-pleasure if his or her sex drive is exceptionally high. If used in this way, maintenance sex can help maintain emotional and physical intimacy in marriage.

As if different sex drives aren't enough, some couples also struggle with different or competing sexual preferences – that is, what sexual activities they wish to perform or enjoy in bed.

Common areas of contention are foreplay, length of lovemaking, oral sex and anal sex, dirty talk, kink and/or extramarital sex, such as swinging or threesomes.

Often (but not always) it is the wife who complains that her husband does not spend enough time in foreplay and, as a result, she has insufficient time to reach the level of arousal she needs to enjoy sex.

The same holds true for the duration of sex. Typically, it is the female partner who desires longer lovemaking. While the occasional "quickie" is great, many women require more to feel sexually satisfied and intimately connected to their mate.

In the landmark book *Human Sexual Response,* sexual researchers Masters and Johnson broke down the human sexual response cycle into a four-stage model of physiological responses. These phases are the excitement phase, the plateau phase, the orgasmic phase and the resolution phase.

Couples who are experiencing conflict over foreplay and duration may find it helpful to educate themselves about these four stages, as they provide valuable insight into an opposite-sex partner's physiological responses to sex and can open a dialogue.

Different sexual preferences also include specific sex acts like oral sex, anal sex, talking dirty in bed and engaging in some type of "kinky" sexplay, such as bondage.

These are touchy subjects to discuss since they often involve issues of personal morality, past experience, self-perception and even fear.

For example, some women say that they would be happy to perform oral sex; however, the oral-sex scenes featured in many pornographic movies are degrading to women, and it can be difficult to see past that.

A wife may require reassurances of love, respect and affection before she is able to do this. Discussing such issues with tact and respect is far preferable to sulking, pressuring or guilt-tripping a partner into doing something she or he doesn't want to do.

All of this notwithstanding, sex is ultimately a subjective, personal experience. Couples should not be surprised if they do not conform to gender expectations.

Instead, they should focus on discovering, respecting and satisfying each other's physiological responses, sexual preferences and limits.

Sex vs. Sleep!

It is often the case that a spouse or spouses will have the best intentions regarding sex. They want to have it, and may even think or talk about it during the day, but once night falls, so too does their energy level.

After cooking supper and cleaning the dishes, helping the kids with their homework and ushering them to bed, packing the next days' lunches, finishing the laundry and/or any work files and so on, many couples find that they're asleep the moment their heads hit the pillow.

They barely have the energy to turn off the bedside lamp, never mind engage in sexual activity. They're just too tired. Not only can this lead to feelings of frustration and neglect, it can cause a couple to feel disconnected.

Nonetheless, sex is a "use it or lose it" type of thing. Quite often, a couple's home life – what they do, when they do it, and how long they do it for – is dictated by force of habit. In such cases, it can be helpful to make sexual intimacy an habitual behavior as well.

Couples can reserve enough energy for regular sex by working together, with the kids, to complete the evening routine as early as possible.

They can also put the kids to bed a little earlier. Even if the kids don't drift off any sooner, the extra quiet time to snuggle in bed can do Mom and Dad a world of good.

Another way to stave off fatigue and have enough energy for sex is to review your overall lifestyle, especially diet and exercise. Are you suppers heavy with carbs? Do you chase it with a glass (or two or three) of wine or beer? Are you and your spouse sedentary?

If so, eating better and exercising can dramatically boost your energy level and your interest in sex. This can also improve your sleeping habits to combat insomnia, so that you are well-rested.

Too stressed for sex?

In addition to fatigue, stress can negatively impact a person's mental and physical well-being. It can also take a profound toll on a couple's sex life, since it is difficult to become aroused when feelings of worry or anxiety are standing in the way.

Some types of stress must be managed at the source – stress about spending, for example, can only be dissipated by better money management. If a job becomes stressful to the point of creating health and family problems, it may be necessary to change work schedules, duties or even work places.

Chronic stress is particularly problematic. Constant and generalized, this type of stress floods the body with "emergency response" hormones like cortisol and adrenaline. The mind and body are never at ease.

Health is compromised. High blood pressure, ulcers, weight gain, eczema, sleep problems, decreased immune response and depression are only a few stress-related effects.

Feelings of happiness are elusive, and relationships are strained. Sex (a stress reliever) falls off the radar, which in turn creates even more stress in the marriage.

One stress-busting idea that can both manage everyday anxiety and encourage intimacy is to transform your bedroom into a sensual sanctuary.

Get rid of anything that isn't related to sex, sleep or the two of you. Move the exercise bike downstairs, put the kids' toys back in their rooms and leave the laptop in your home office.

Replace your worn, scratchy bedsheets with satin sheets and invest in a luxurious duvet. Take down the cheap vertical blinds and hang rich, light-blocking drapery over the windows.

Paint over your boring beige walls with a deep, sensual color like red, purple, emerald or blue. Or go the other route and aim for a clean look, with light-colored walls and crisp white bedding.

Toss some variously-textured pillows and cushions on the bed. To complete the transformation, replace harsh white lightbulbs with soft, glare-free bulbs, burn an aromatherapy candle and experiment with a sound machine. These block out distracting background noise and fill the room with relaxing nature sounds.

Another intimacy issue is the "love vs. sex" debate. When intimacy problems arise, some couples fall into debate over which is more important or meaningful – love or sex?

Instead of agreeing upon the importance of both and trying to incorporate both into their marriage, they allow their competing ideas to widen the distance between them, reducing both love and sex.

When this happens, one or both spouses may begin to moralize and come across as superior. For example, a wife might say, "All you want is sex, which makes you shallow." This will most likely lead to anger and defensiveness on the part of the other spouse.

One or both spouses may also try to persuade, guilt-trip or manipulate the other. For example, a husband might say, "If you loved me, you'd have sex with me." These approaches do nothing but create sour, antagonistic feelings that compromise both sex and love.

The truth is, sex and love in marriage are two sides of the same coin. They are of equal value, even though their degree, frequency, scope and relative importance can change, depending on a couple's age, moods, life events, focus and so on.

Love + Sex = True Intimacy

Marriage can be defined as a romantic friendship between two people who have committed to spend their lives together.

When it comes to love and sex, the whole is greater than the sum of its parts. Pitting those parts against each other does more harm than good. It is a gross misuse of energy.

Instead, couples must focus on how love and sex are interconnected. They must think about how they support, strengthen and bring greater meaning to each other.

After all, it is the unique dynamic between love and sex that distinguishes a romantic or marriage relationship from every other relationship in a person's life.

Although often shameful for a spouse to admit, he or she may at times feel sexually unattracted to a partner, even when deep feelings of love remain.

It may be that the other spouse has undergone some kind of body change, such as pregnancy, weight gain or loss, illness, hair loss, et cetera.

It may also be that the other spouse has "let themselves go" and is no longer taking care of his or her appearance in terms of dress, body care or fitness.

Is it time to rekindle
the sparks of attraction?

Here are few tips to reignite attraction:

• Remember how your partner looked, and how you desired him or her, when you first met. Ask him or her on "a date." Revisit an old photo album or carry a picture of your spouse looking his or her best, and think of all the things you have gone through together.

• Suggest a fun "couple's makeover" to your spouse, where you both challenge yourselves to update your look and take better care of yourselves. This shines the spotlight on you, not just your partner.

• Do something new and different together, whether it's white water rafting or learning a new language. The endorphins and excitement of a new adventure can rub off on your relationship.

• Think about the ways that you used to arouse and please your partner, both in and out of the bedroom, and start doing them again. This may motivate your spouse to put in the same effort.

- Do not compare your spouse to other people. Not only is it cruel and unfair, it can reinforce your feelings of dissatisfaction and cause feelings of resentment, insecurity and self-consciousness in your spouse.

- Challenge your ideas about what is attractive. Are they superficial or self-centered? Focus on both the physical and character traits that you find most appealing about your partner.

- Remind yourself that physical attraction comes and goes over the years, as does the feeling of love itself. You may not be attracted to your partner at this moment, but the feeling may return sooner than you think. Remember that, next time, it may be your partner who is no longer attracted to you. How would you want him or her to behave?

A spouse may also lose sexual attraction to a partner if that partner comes across as a lazy or selfish lover. Perhaps the partner doesn't know any better or assumes that all is well.

Perhaps he or she doesn't have the motivation – for whatever reason – to expend the energy it takes to be an enthusiastic or thoughtful lover. Perhaps he or she has simply fallen into a rut and needs a gentle reminder to bring a little more to the party.

Regardless, sex is a two-player game. And if one player is doing all the work or making all the game-winning plays, it's only a matter of time until he or she either throws in the towel or finds a better playmate.

If you feel that you are doing all the work in bed, you should start with a positive approach. Tell your partner that you miss his or her "signature move," that twist, tweak or thrust that he or she used to do so well.

If your partner doesn't have a lot of moves to draw from, think about purchasing a sex guide that focuses on sexual techniques and positions. Take the initiative and bring it into your bedroom in a spirit of playfulness, not criticism.

If your partner doesn't seem to have the motivation or energy to pleasure you, ask yourself why. How do you talk to and treat him or her outside of the bedroom? Is he or she still up after you've gone to bed, perhaps putting the kids to bed or folding laundry?

When a spouse feels underappreciated or overworked, he or she often brings those negative feelings to bed. It may be that you need to improve the quality of your overall interactions before the sex improves.

Unfortunately, some lazy and selfish partners are just that – lazy and selfish. Chances are, if your partner behaves like this in bed, he or she is not much different in other areas of your life together. In such instances, the problem isn't really a sexual one and your focus should be on improving the relationship (not just sex) and ensuring that your needs are met.

Boring sex can also lead to a loss of sexual attraction and motivation. It can rob a couple of sexual enjoyment, reduce the "playfulness" in their marriage, lead to sexual apathy, lower the frequency of sex in the relationship and even make them question their commitment and love for each other.

Spice it Up!

Fortunately, the sexual "spice it up" industry is teeming with options, from sex toys and guides to erotica and romantic getaways, and everything in between; however, sexual enthusiasm remains the biggest antidote to bedroom boredom. When one spouse shows an active interest in sex – and in the other spouse! – his or her enthusiastic spirit can spread to the other spouse.

Finally, a quick note about pornography. Nowadays, the most explicit of images are only a click away due to the online porn industry. The availability and variety of online pornography taps into the most intense of human instincts – the sex drive – and can ignite a plethora of sexual problems between intimate partners.

Yet not all pornography is created equal. There is couple-focused, female-friendly adult material that steers clear of the "barely legal" and degrading, sometimes disgusting content that turns so many women – and men, for that matter – off porn.

This type of higher-quality pornography can help couples with arousal and variety, so long as its use does not become too frequent or necessary for arousal. It can also give them ideas for new things to try in bed.

In cases where one spouse wants to watch porn but the other is less eager, having a conversation about content, quality and frequency may therefore help couples find the type of adult material that they are both comfortable with.

That being said, there are people who are opposed to porn, in any form or frequency. If an individual knew this about their partner before marriage, it is unfair to expect or demand them to change after marriage.

In some cases, a person will become anti-porn because of a partner's porn habits. A wife, for example, may want to restrict all porn usage because of a husband "porn habit."

If her husband is pleasuring himself most or all of the time by masturbating to pornography, he is withholding both the physical and emotional intimacy that is wife is entitled to receive from him. This can only lead to resentment.

Unfortunately, many couples who struggle with a pornography problem focus on the wrong thing. For example, a man might say, "All guys watch porn. You need to lighten up. I don't do it that much."

To this, his wife might reply, "You watch it all the time. You're sick." Instead of talking about how porn is affecting their relationship and self-perception, they focus on their own desires or assumptions, often marginalizing and insulting their partner in the process.

Pornography addiction is generally described as an overuse/abuse of porn that leads a person to experience negative consequences.

Marriage problems – such as a loss of sexual intimacy – is certainly a negative consequence.

When discussing problematic porn usage, couples will fare better if they focus on the negative effects the porn is having on their relationship and respective self-perceptions, rather than trying to win the porn argument in a moral sense or simply get their way.

By focusing on porn's impact on the marriage and on how it makes the more porn-resistant partner feel about herself or himself, a couple creates a loving, respectful and reassuring environment in which to talk about this touchy topic.

Such an environment is far more likely to lead to a mutual agreement on how pornography and erotica is to be used in the marriage.

For example, one couple may decide that only female-friendly pornography will be viewed together, and only on "special occasions" like romantic getaways.

Another couple may decide that partners can watch whatever they want, whenever they want, so long as it is done in private – outside of the bedroom – and does not reduce their sexual frequency or pleasure. Still another couple may decide they can watch pornography only while masturbating.

The point is, once a couple is able to discuss the pornography issue with genuine respect and insight into their partner's point of view, while at the same time acknowledging how the porn issue is impacting the marriage, they are far more likely to resolve this problem in a way that works for both spouses.

Those struggling with sex and intimacy issues should focus on the following strategies in Part III: Day 4 (physical & emotional affection); Day 9 (show desire); Day 13 (appreciation): Day 16 (fun & laughter); Day 25 (fight familiarity); and Day 26 (sex & intimacy).

Parenting Issues

Even parents with the best of intentions can critique each other's parenting skills or habits. Sometimes that's a good thing. It may be that dad is spending a bit too much time in the garage lately, and mom is yelling a bit too loudly these days.

Parents are partners and, as long as their concerns are voiced with respect and a collaborative spirit, they can be a fantastic team and a blessing to a child.

When parents disagree, their children don't need to know about it. Disagreements should be discussed in private, behind closed doors.

If parents want to acknowledge or apologize to their kids for a parenting mistake (everyone makes them), they should do this together, without singling out one parent out as the wrongdoer.

Spouses should also ensure that children treat the other parent with respect. This shows kids that their parents are on the same team but, even more, that they are two people who really love and honor each other.

More serious parenting problems often arise when one parent believes that his or her way is "the right way," and tries to persuade or even bully a spouse into parenting in a certain way.

For example, one spouse may believe that a child should not get an allowance for helping out with household chores, while the other spouse believes an allowance is motivational.

This may lead to open conflict between spouses. As bad, it can cause one spouse to "give up" and adopt the other spouse's parenting approach, just to avoid a fight. This can only lead to resentment. People want and need the freedom to parent their own children.

It takes two to parent. The maternal parent brings certain things to child-raising, as does the paternal parent. They bring different emotions, perspectives, qualities and behaviors. They are different things to the child at different times. When one spouse restricts the natural parenting of his or her spouse, he or she robs the child of an invaluable resource.

As bad, when one spouse restricts the natural parenting of the other spouse, he or she inadvertently causes that marginalized spouse to feel less invested in the family unit. He or she may feel like an outsider in his or her own home. And that's never a good thing.

The same is true of same-sex spouses. Each partner brings a wealth of unique abilities, personality and experience to his or her role as parent, and a child is much poorer for the lack of those things.

Parents must realize that they are of equal value. They must also realize that a "united front" is absolutely essential when it comes to parenting.

A common reason that parents lose their united front is because they turn their relationship into a child-centered one. That is, their children – rather than their love – become the focus and purpose of their partnership. They invest all their time, money and energy into their kids' activities and events, marginalizing the importance of their loving friendship and romance.

Have a united front – and
remember the value of romantic love …

All parents love their children; however, they must acknowledge that romantic love also has value. When parents prioritize and demonstrate their love for each other, they show their children what it takes to make marriage work. A united front isn't just a way to parent. It's a way to live life as loving, intimate partners.

In some family units – particularly those where the parents are unhappy or do not have a united front – there arises a destructive "divide and conquer" mentality between family members, with certain parents and certain children forming hurtful alliances that chip away at family solidarity.

For example, a mother may undermine her husband's parental authority by allowing her teen-age daughter to break curfew. The mother's intention is to befriend her child and make her happy; however, the net result is that the child begins to see the mother as an ally and the father as an enemy. Not only does this compromise the couple's marriage, it robs the child of a strong father figure.

Another example: A father doesn't let his wife read their young son's text messages. His intent is to win his son's trust; however, the net result is that he presents the mother as a subordinate parent who cannot be trusted. This causes the wife to feel resentment toward her husband and to feel excluded from her child's life. It also robs the son of a mother's comfort and insight, and sets a poor example of marriage, partnership and co-parenting.

In both examples, the child learns that the parents can be turned against each other for his or her benefit. These are just two examples of shifting alliances. Within a family unit, there are any number of ways that parents, children and siblings can take sides or gang up on each other.

If you feel this is happening in your family unit, you and your spouse need to have a serious conversation about what "family" means to you. More importantly, what do you want it to mean to your kids?

Instead of modeling divisiveness and disloyalty, show your kids what it means for a family to stick together. Put the family unit on a pedestal. Teach them that family members "have each other's back" and that they don't play favorites. If they learn this lesson, they are far more likely to enjoy the countless benefits of a successful family life when they marry and have their own kids.

In-Law Problems

Mothers-in-law have an undeservedly bad reputation. Most mothers-in-law are fantastic. They are helpful, respectful and accepting even when the person who marries their "baby" is not the person they might have chosen. Nonetheless, they want their child to be happy and they go out of their way to maintain a good relationship with the person who is making that happen.

Unfortunately, other mothers-in-law deserve their "monster-in-law" reputation. They are jealous, scheming and petty. Sometimes they are even dangerous, since they can undermine their child's marriage and family life.

While there are cases of husbands not getting along with mothers-in-law, the typical battle is mother-in-law vs. wife, so that's what we'll look at first.

In such cases, it is important for the wife to be as compassionate as possible, and to take a critical look at her own behavior before blaming the mother-in-law for everything. Any mother who loves her son can sympathize with what it must be like to see him love, prefer and rely upon a woman that isn't her.

A wife should also try to empathize with her husband. It is stressful and emotionally agonizing for a man to be caught between the two women he loves so deeply – his mother and his wife.

A wife should understand that he won't want to confront his mother or criticize her. She is the woman who loved him first, and they have a history that his wife wasn't part of.

For these reasons, a wife may wish to establish her own relationship with her mother-in-law, without always asking her husband to chastise his mother for small and possibly innocent transgressions. It is vital to set and enforce boundaries in a respectful but firm way.

For example, a wife whose mother-in-law critiques her parenting might have to address the matter head on by saying something like, "I know you love your grandkids and want the best for them. There are many times I will ask for your advice because I know it's valuable, but I need to find my own way to parent. It would help me if you could bite your tongue unless it's something that you find really important."

This approach does three things:

a) It acknowledges the mother-in-law's needs and emotions, making her feel appreciated and validated.

b) It lets her know that her behaviour is not acceptable

c) It sets a specific, understandable and fair boundary

Note that these messages are delivered in a relatively friendly manner. The mother-in-law even has polite permission to cross the boundary and speak if it's "really important" to her. By respectfully leaving her some control, it is more likely that she will listen to these messages and not abuse the privilege.

Of course, the husband's involvement is necessary if the mother-in-law is stubborn, clueless or has ill intentions. When it comes down to it, a husband **must** choose his wife and family over his mother.

If his mother tends to fictionalize events or "take things personally," he should be the person to speak with her about boundaries and the way she is treating his wife.

Let's assume that a wife has done her best to get along with her mother-in-law, but the conflict between them is nonetheless escalating. Perhaps the mother-in-law is insulting, deceptive or mean-spirited.

Here are a few tips to help manage this difficult situation:

- Get some emotional distance. Don't set yourself up for disappointment or frustration by reaching out to her, hoping things will change or trying to fix the situation. Get on with life and try to put her out of your mind.

- Get some physical distance. Don't feel obligated to attend every family event. If things deteriorate, suggest a move to a new city. People are better behaved around those they don't see much.

- Be aware of how your mother-in-law "pushes your buttons," and share this information with your spouse.

Before an event with your mother-in-law, discuss ways that you and your spouse can work together to manage your triggers when she is around.

- Be honest. If your mother-in-law is dishing out guilt, criticism or bad manners, call her on it. Do this with tact and honesty.

Do not take her bait by responding in anger or storming off, and never talk badly about her to others. You'll look like the bad guy.

- Keep your spouse in mind. Even when you're angry, remember that she is your spouse's mother. You can set and enforce boundaries without resorting to name-calling, temper tantrums or character assassination. Those things aren't necessary and, even if you feel justified, they can hurt your marriage. Don't give a troublesome mother-in-law that satisfaction!

- Ask for your spouse's support. Let your husband know how difficult it is to get along with his mother – although he probably already knows this! –and how much it means to you to know that he appreciates your efforts.

A wife can usually "suck it up" a lot more if her husband acknowledges and appreciates what she is doing for him and for their family.

In cases where it is the husband who has rocky relations with his mother-in-law, these same general principles can apply.

While disputes involving fathers-in-law aren't are prevalent as those involving mothers-in-law, they certainly do exist. A conservative, religious father-in-law may not welcome his liberal, atheist daughter-in-law into the fold.

At the same time, a young husband may not appreciate his father-in-law rushing in to rescue "daddy's little girl" every time her car's engine makes a funny noise.

Spouses must prioritize and protect their partner, and other members of the family must see this preferential treatment in action.

A person who does not prioritize and protect his or her spouse – whether he is a "mama's boy" or she is "daddy's little girl" – is misplacing the love and loyalty that defines marriage. He or she cannot enjoy an intimate partnership with another human being.

To be sure, some real-life family dynamics rival the drama, intrigue and politics of a soap opera. There are shifting alliances, judgments and scheming.

There is juicy gossip, rumor and accusation. There are snubs and cold shoulders galore. A person can't turn his or her back without finding a knife sticking out of it.

It's easy to be drawn into petty yet destructive family dramas. And once in, things can quickly get ugly. Worse, this private ugliness is often made public when sparring in-laws post their battle statuses on social media sites.

For example, it is all too common for an angry person to post "My brother's wife is an evil bitch!" or "My sister-in-law is a nosey, lying, back-stabbing whore!" on a social media site, airing their dirty laundry in cyberspace, slandering a family member and annihilating any chance of salvaging the relationship.

Unfortunately, this type of nonsense has a way of causing marital problems, as a spouse finds himself or herself caught between a partner and a sibling.

A three-part approach can help you stay out of family infighting:

a) **Retreat from the battle.** After all, this isn't the hill you want your marriage to die on.

b) **Mind your own business.** If it doesn't involve you – well, it doesn't involve you.

c) **Be supportive but don't take sides.** High-drama families are pros at turning people against one another. Take the high ground. Such discretion and distance can prevent their infighting from causing a rift between you and your spouse.

In situations where an in-law or other extended family member seems to attack you on a personal level, you can use some of the same tips used to manage a difficult mother-in-law.

These include getting emotional and physical distance, knowing how this person triggers you, being honest and tactfully "calling them out" on their behavior, and enlisting your spouse's support.

There's just one thing that doesn't work: Trying to beat them at their own game.

Not only will you lose and put yourself through untold and unnecessary stress and anger, you may damage your marriage and family life in the process.

Some people just aren't worth it. Limit contact, put them "on ignore" and get on with life.

Unfortunately, some in-law conflicts become so severe that an estrangement – that is, cutting all contact – may be warranted. Although a last resort, such action may be required when an in-law makes false accusations that threaten the integrity of the marriage or family unit, behaves with cruelty or malice, shows unpredictable or dangerous behavior or threatens the safety or well-being of family members, including children.

An in-law who does more harm than good may need his or her walking papers, whether temporarily or permanently. In such cases, it must be the spouse with the primary or blood relationship who makes the break and explains why it is happening.

The Ex-Wife / Ex-Husband

The high rate of divorce makes it statistically possible that either you or your spouse has an ex-spouse. If this previous marriage was without children, there is little conceivable reason why ex-spouses should remain in meaningful or frequent contact, particularly if that contact is problematic in the current marriage; however, contact is unavoidable if they have children together.

The types of relationships that exist between ex-spouses, and between ex-spouses and current spouses, run the gamut from true friendship to total enmity.

An amicable relationship for the sake of the children should be the minimum goal.

Regardless of the mess adults sometimes make of their relationships, they at least have choice and power – children of divorce have neither.

Worse, they are the ones who suffer the consequences of divorce long after the papers have been signed and their parents have moved on to new relationships.

A married person who has children from a previous relationship often finds himself or herself in a tricky spot.

To ensure contact and good relations with his or her kids, he or she must maintain an amicable relationship with the ex-spouse. To keep the peace, he or she may occasionally "let things slide" with a previous partner and put up with unreasonable behavior.

This can cause problems when the current spouse misinterprets a partner's accommodating behavior as weakness or as evidence that the partner is still invested in the previous relationship, perhaps holding onto feelings for the previous partner.

In such instances, it is essential for the spouse with the ex-partner to reassure the current spouse that his or her behavior is motivated by the need to maintain access to his or her children, rather than unresolved feelings for the ex.

Alienating an ex-spouse can lead to all kinds of headaches in terms of visitation. It is sometimes easier to "suck it up" and put up with a difficult ex-spouse than run the risk of losing easy access to one's kids.

Indeed, much conflict involving ex-spouses is due to the current spouse's fear that his or her partner's loyalties still lie with the previous partner. A spouse might say that his or her spouse is "at the ex's beck and call."

While ex-spouses do need to cut the cord on aspects of their relationship that do not involve their children, this can be a slippery slope. For example, what if an ex-wife finds herself stranded on the side of the road in a snow storm? Is it appropriate for her to call her ex-husband, or can she only call if the children are in the vehicle with her?

Unfortunately, there is no hard and fast rule when it comes to ex-spouses with whom a person has children. This is a reality that current spouses must face.

In the end, common sense and realism must prevail. A man should rescue his children's mother from a snow storm regardless of whether the kids are in the car; however, he doesn't have to take her out for dinner afterward! In fact, he would be wise to arrive home with a bouquet of roses for his current wife.

When it comes to managing tricky ex-spouse / current spouse relationships, there are two general concepts to keep in mind:

1. Respect. A new spouse must respect the fact that his or her partner has loyalties to previous children, not to the previous partner. A spouse with an ex-partner must also respect the new partner's feelings and behave accordingly.

2. Reassurance. A spouse with an ex-partner must reassure the new partner that his or her loyalties lie with the current marriage.

These two simple concepts – mutual respect and reassurance – can be applied to any situation of perceived divided loyalties, including in-law conflicts.

The fact is, a marriage can only survive and thrive when both spouses feel they are at the top of the other's priority list, far above ex-partners and in-laws.

Spouses who do not send this message loudly and clearly, and who do not stand by their words in terms of behavior, are destined for marital disaster.

Creating and enforcing boundaries with family members and ex-spouses is not easy; however, it has to be done. Unless a current spouse is acting with malice or is deliberately being disrespectful to the other relationships in a partner's life, he or she must come before parents, siblings or extended family, and ex-spouses.

Because setting these kinds of boundaries is so difficult to do on a practical level, it is ideal if spouses can work together to brainstorm ways they can create and enforce fair, realistic limits.

By working as a team and supporting each other, a couple can actually turn this potentially divisive problem into a way to strengthen their partnership. Adopt a proud "it's us against the world" attitude, so that you can learn to face adversity together.

Even better, try to have a sense of humor about the whole thing. That's easy to say, isn't it? But it's also true.

By turning your "In-Laws & Out-Laws" tragedy into a comedy, you and your spouse may find yourselves laughing rather than fighting. Remember that, when it comes down to it, your marriage and family are far more important than any in-law drama.

Blended Families & Step-Children

While some blended families work great, many have serious problems. This is for a number of reasons. Some adults who re-marry and "blend" their respective children assume that their children are more accepting of the situation than they really are.

Other adults assume that the blended family will be similar to the first-marriage family and mistakenly expect similar dynamics.

Still other adults "demand" respect from non-biological children. And some adults, unfortunately, have resentment toward their non-biological children, whether in terms of their behavior, how much money they cost or their very presence.

Poor preparation, ineffective communication and unrealistic expectations also lead to problems in new and existing blended families.

It is baffling how many adults expect to move in together, with their respective children in tow, and effortlessly mesh into one big, happy family. It doesn't work like that.

As adults, you might be ready to start a new life. Your kids, however, might be having a hard time keeping up with the changes that you are effecting in their lives.

They might dislike their new home, situation, step-parent and step-siblings. They might have all kinds of emotions that, as a young person, they cannot deal with. These might include fear, stress, guilt, sadness, anger, helplessness, resentment and so on. Don't take it personally if your children and/or step-children show less enthusiasm for the process than you'd like.

You cannot force a person – whether a child or an adult – to like a certain situation or emotionally react in a certain way. The best you can do is to talk to them honestly, and address their emotions, needs, concerns and preferences.

All members of a new blended family must feel heard, respected and valued.

All members must have a voice and sense of control over their own lives.

All members must feel wanted and welcomed, and that they belong there.

This is especially so for children. If you as an adult do not feel wanted or welcomed, you have the maturity, life experience and interpersonal skills to improve your situation, and to cope until it does improve. Children do not.

Whether your blended family is a new arrangement or a current situation, you and your spouse can take some important, immediate measures to improve its chances of success and the quality of your home life. These include the following.

Tips for blended family success:

• Keep your expectations in check. Aim for a cooperative coexistence. Anything better than that is a bonus. Be patient and don't push.

- Open a dialogue to discuss roles and rules. This discussion should take place in a respectful, collaborative way that takes everyone's feelings, wants and needs into account.

- Have a strategy to address and resolve conflict between all family members. Finding common ground can help people connect and collaborate. The strategy presented on Day 30 (resolve conflict) in Part III can provide a framework for this process.

- Ask the children to contribute to the conversation. They need an opportunity to express themselves freely.

How do they feel about all of this? What are they worried about? Do they have any suggestions that might make the transition easier or more appealing to them?

There is a simple strategy in Part III, on Day 20 (empathy),that can be very useful to help you understand where everyone is coming from. It is particularly useful if you are dealing with younger kids or teenagers that aren't willing to open up.

- Work with your spouse. Children should see that you have a loving, cooperative relationship and that you are doing your best to "blend" various lives into a new family unit, the whole of which is greater than the sum of its parts. They should see good humor and good intentions.

- Create rituals to give the new family unit its own identity. These can be cheesy science-fiction movie nights, backyard astronomy, dirt-biking or Saturday morning cartoons and cereal.

Don't underestimate the bonding power of having a fun home and family life. The family that plays together stays together, and that goes for nuclear and blended families alike.

Aesop's fable of the North Wind and the Sun teaches a wonderful, wise lesson that spouses seeking to blend a family should learn well:

One day, two old friends – the North Wind and the Sun – were arguing about who was stronger. They saw a man walking below, wearing a jacket and a hat. The North Wind said, "I am stronger. I can get the jacket off that man sooner than you can."

And so the North Wind blew and blew and blew. His cold wind tore the leaves from the trees, ripped kites out of children's hands and blew the man's hat off his head.

The man lowered his head and wrapped his jacket even tighter around him. The North Wind blew even harder but, try as he might, he could not get the jacket off the man.

The Sun said, "Let me try, my friend."

And so the Sun shone and shone. The trees rested and the children ran across the grass to find their kites. The man raised his face to the Sun and felt its warmth on his face. Smiling, he took off his jacket and threw it over his shoulder as he continued along his way.

You get the idea, right? Warmth is better than coldness. Persuasion is better than force. You get more flies with honey than vinegar.

They may be clichés, but they're also the living truth. It's a law of human nature that people respond better, faster and more sincerely when someone reaches out to them with a loving hand, rather than trying to grab them with an unfriendly one.

This warm, persuasive approach is definitely the way to go with step-children, especially to buck an unflattering stereotype: The controlling, bitchy stepmother and the mean, bullying stepfather.

These evil archetypes resent their step-children and would give anything for them to go live with the other parent or disappear. Fortunately, most mature, moral adults do not harbor such antipathy toward their spouse's children. Even if they do, they are able to behave appropriately.

It may be that your step-children are particularly challenging. Perhaps they have emotional issues or behavioral problems. Perhaps they have different personalities than you.

Perhaps they're difficult to like and married life would be easier and more fun without them around. But they are around and you must learn to live together.

There is a general rule of thumb for step-parents who are struggling to get along with step-children: **Be a friend, not a parent.** You are not this child's biological parent, and behaving as though you are will only make things worse.

For example, child discipline – especially in new or struggling blended families – should be the domain of the biological parent only.

This doesn't mean the step-parent cannot appropriately and respectfully enforce the rules (i.e. curfew times, homework before video games); however, if the child starts to resist the rules, it is the biological parent's role to get him or her back in line.

Check out the following ideas to improve the step-parent / step-child relationship.

Tips for a good step-parent / step-child relationship:

- Respect the non-residential biological parent (your step-child's mom or dad) and encourage contact between her or him and your step-child.

Help your step-child shop for the non-residential parent's birthday gifts, etc.

- Use what interests your step-child (music, movies, superheroes, clothes) to bridge the distance between you and him or her. Form your own unique friendship with your step-child and find shared interests.

- Fill a void that you see in your step-child's life. For example, does he or she want to learn how to play an instrument or do better in school? Does he or she need someone to talk to, shop with or encourage him or her?

- Create a household where your step-child's friends, other family members and pets are welcomed with open arms and treated with kindness and respect.

- Create a fun, supportive household for all members. Make your house a place that your step-children want to come home to.

There is another type of common but dysfunctional dynamic that plays out in blended families where both spouses have brought children into the marriage.

Parental instinct kicks in, often unnecessarily, until spouses feel that they must "protect" their children from the other spouse and the other spouse's children.

This leads to defensiveness and hostility in the home as spouses, and their kids, must learn to live in a battle zone. Soon, everyone begins to feel that their "family members" are enemies, not allies.

But parents are not just protective of their children. They are also proud of them. There is productive pride, like when a child works hard to improve a math score.

There is also unproductive pride, like when one spouse feels that his or her child is "better" or more deserving than the other spouse's child.

This can cause a spouse to give blatant and sometimes obnoxious special treatment to their own child. The situation is made worse when spouses don't connect with each other's kids.

For example, it's not okay for your child to do five-minutes per week of chores – because he just gets so tired! – while your spouse's child is expected to do an hour. It's not okay to overlook your child's toys on the floor while criticizing your spouse's child for leaving crumbs on the counter.

It not okay for your teenager to borrow the family car whenever he likes, while your spouse's teenager has to take the bus. It's not okay to let your adult child live indefinitely in the basement suite while forbidding your spouse's adult child from moving in.

It is essential that one set of household expectations and rules exist, and are equally enforced, for all children living in the home. Of course, common sense must dictate the particulars. If one spouse has a toddler and the other spouse has a teenager, the expectations and rules must be appropriate to their ages and abilities.

The goal is fairness and equal treatment. That can be achieved even in homes where there are children of various ages and abilities. It's your attitude, not your logistics, that count.

It may be that one spouse's child is more problematic than the other spouse's. It may be tempting for the other spouse to criticize or complain about the child, perhaps even comparing a partner's "problem child" to his or her own "perfect child."

Again, this can trigger a spouse's parental instinct as he or she rises up to protect and defend his or her child from the other spouse.

This can destroy a marriage. After all, people expect a spouse to love them, support them and care about the things they love. A spouse who instead attacks the things they adore isn't much of a life partner. It's just a matter of time until the marriage becomes seriously strained.

Instead of slamming a spouse's problematic child, show your support. Turn the issue inside-out.

Rather than letting this situation undermine your partnership (which it will do), use it as an opportunity to show your spouse what a caring, competent and committed partner you are.

The better you treat your spouse's children, the more your spouse will love you!

In that way, your marriage grows stronger, not weaker. The truth is, decent parents will always stand by their children, whether those kids are problematic or perfect.

It is also common in blended-family situations for one spouse's children to live in the marital home, while the other spouse's children reside elsewhere with the other biological parent.

This can lead to intense feelings of guilt, betrayal and sadness on the part of the non-residential biological parent. It can also make it difficult for him or her to bond with step-children.

In such cases, the spouse whose children reside in the marital home must not push or guilt a spouse into bonding with his or her step-children. While the spouse does have to treat his or her step-children with friendship, respect and kindness, they are not "replacements" for his or her biological children.

It's perfectly natural for people to love their biological children more than their step-children. If you don't like that, take it up with Mother Nature.

To strengthen the marriage and the blended family unit, the spouse whose children reside in the marital home should strive to give his or her spouse's children a "presence" in the home.

This might mean hanging pictures of them, displaying their artwork, talking about them during supper and taking the initiative to invite them over and include them in family events.

Give your spouse's children a "presence" in your home.

The better a non-residential parent feels about his or her relationship with his or her biological children, the easier it will be for him or her to establish a good relationship with his or her step-children.

It is also a common blended family situation that spouses, both of whom have their own children, go on to have a child together. This can sometimes make existing children feel unwanted or less loved. Not only do they struggle with feelings of fear, insecurity, jealousy and sadness, they may feel uncertain about their place – both in the home and in their parents' hearts.

Again, it is important to maintain an open, age-appropriate dialogue with all children so that they understand they are loved, valued and adored for who they are as unique individuals. Children must always have an opportunity to express their emotions, needs and fears and have those addressed.

Keep in mind that kids often make negative assumptions about themselves. In all circumstances – and especially when you are bringing new half-siblings into the picture – you must reassure them that they have a permanent, unique spot in your heart and life.

Finally, remember to practice what you preach. Ensure that all children are treated fairly in terms of expectations and rules. It does no good to tell a child that he or she is "just as loved" as another child in your life, but then favor the other child. Your new children do not trump your previous children.

It often happens that spouses who have children from previous relationships manage to get along very well – until money is mentioned. People can bite like snakes when they feel a hand slide into their pocketbook.

Kids are expensive. Couples in second or subsequent marriages must plan and provide for their financial future; however, they must be alive to the cost of raising both their, and their spouse's, children.

Again, equal treatment must apply. If your daughter wants to take dance and your spouse's son wants to take karate, it's either both or neither. The activities, belongings and quality of life must be similar for all children who live under the same roof. This is tough for some people to accept – but what kind of family would have it any other way?

Child support payments can be a particularly sore area. Typically, the step-parent resents what his or her spouse's child "is costing them." The step-parent may inject himself or herself into the payment schedule, complaining that it is excessive or railing against additional expenses (i.e. a contribution toward a teenager's high-school trip to Europe or drivers' training lessons).

When it comes to child support payments for minor children, whether court mandated or agreed upon by the biological parents, and including additional payments, it is inappropriate for the step-parent to get involved. Doing so can upset the relationship that ex-spouses have developed to co-parent their children after divorce. That is selfish and short-sighted.

If you are a spouse who is unhappy with your partner's child-support payments, you should remember that you entered into the relationship will full knowledge of the children. It will better serve everyone if you now put your financial acumen to use in other areas. You might not like this message, but it is one that could very well save your marriage.

And wouldn't you rather save your marriage than save a buck? Think long-term. Put your marriage first.

*Don't let the cost of raising
kids cost you your marriage.*

Similarly, if you have kids from a previous relationship and your current spouse is complaining about your child-support payments, you must be firm: "My child support payments are not changing at this time and, unless you have something supportive to say, they are not to be discussed." This is one of those marital issues where the "hard line" is warranted. You cannot allow a self-focused or unreasonable partner to compromise the parent-child relationship.

This holds true even if spouses have gone on to have children together. Once again, the financial needs of "new" children and family units do not trump previous ones. Parents have a responsibility to love and pay for all their children. And children are far more in-tune to preferential treatment than you might think.

A Belligerent, Critical or Defensive Spouse

Even after the years I've spent as a couples' mediator and the countless clients I've seen, I am still amazed – and not in a good way – by how some spouses treat each other.

They scream insults, swear, name-call, bully and throw adult temper tantrums that make the average two-year-old look like a model of maturity and self-restraint.

Even when gently challenged on their behavior by a well-meaning spouse, they fly off the handle and become defensive. Quite honestly, these people should be ashamed of themselves.

Be honest with yourself: Am I describing your behavior?

If so, you can erupt in rage or indignation as you normally do, or you can do something positive to change your life and your marriage before you end up a bitter, lonely, regretful human being without one person who will visit you in your golden years.

Your spouse, or more likely your trail of ex-spouses, won't bother to spend time with you. Neither will your grown children, who vowed to never speak to you again once they had the means to move out of the miserable home they shared with you during what should have been the joyful, carefree days of their childhood.

If you are willing to change, I suggest you begin by reading the strategies presented on Day 1 (voice tone), Day 5 (get to the root of arguments); Day 20 (empathy), Day 22 (respect), Day 27 (humility), Day 28 (learn to communicate) and Day 29 (manage intense emotion and anger) in Part III of this book.

Again, be honest with yourself: You know that anger or "a mean streak" is robbing you of happiness. You may even feel ashamed of it. You know it is putting your long-term relationships at risk. Do the right thing and face up to it. Take steps to free yourself from the grip of anger. Your life will be better for it.

Perhaps it is your spouse that is displaying these kinds of behaviors. In this case, I must issue a caveat: if you have concerns about the emotional well-being or physical safety of yourself or your children, you have a moral and legal obligation to contact the appropriate resource, whether the police, a lawyer and/or a mental health practitioner.

Belligerent spouses aren't just unpleasant, they can be unpredictable and dangerous, and often turn abusive. No marriage in the world is worth you or your children suffering harm, or worse. Do not rely upon this or any self-help book. Reach out to a therapist or counselor and/or the authorities.

But how to cope with a belligerent spouse in less serious cases? How to get him or her to stop swearing, name-calling or blowing-up over nothing so that you can stop spending your life walking on eggshells?

How to change this pattern of control and submission?

After all, spouses who fly off the handle in anger, defensiveness or criticism receive a self-serving kickback – they get their way! Don't expect them to easily let go of that kind of control.

The best way to deal with belligerence is to stop it from becoming a tolerated behavior in the marriage in the first place. That is, the first time you see belligerent behavior, you walk away and make it abundantly clear that you simply will not put up with it.

People will treat you as well or
as poorly as you allow them to.

The hard truth is, some people will treat you as poorly as you allow them to. Absolutely nothing is as effective as showing a partner, from day one of your relationship, that you will not tolerate belligerence, angry outbursts, obnoxious defensiveness or self-righteous criticism.

I have had many spouses in my office who will say that their husband or wife has been bullying and name-calling them for years. Yet the spouse continues to put up with the behavior, thus allowing it to continue.

A runaway train doesn't stop unless something derails it. That something might have to be you. If you have emotional or psychological issues that are preventing you from asserting yourself or recognizing that belligerent behavior is utterly unacceptable, I strongly encourage you to seek the guidance of a mental health practitioner.

Not long ago, I saw a female client who complained that her husband never thanked her for running most of the errands and doing most of the parenting duties for his biological daughter who lived with them. He showed no appreciation and treated her more like the hired help than a wife.

On the odd occasion that she couldn't drive her step-daughter to dance class, her husband would "freak out" and throw a temper tantrum, complete with profanity and calling his wife a "lazy bitch." He would rant about how busy he was, slam doors and yell so loudly that the neighbors could hear. When I asked her how long this had been going on, she said five years.

When behavior is this entrenched, it is very difficult to change. It can be done, but it requires humility and a truly willing spirit on the part of the belligerent spouse. It also requires self-respect and self-assuredness on the part of the belittled spouse. It requires determination and persistence on the part of both spouses.

Open a dialogue...

To begin, spouses must be able to have a heart-to-heart conversation about this belligerent behavior and express their emotions, fears and insight about it.

Timing is important in this regard. It is pointless to try and talk about nasty behavior while the nastiness is happening. In fact, it can be destructive.

At that point, the situation has escalated to the point that people are too emotional. They're not thinking straight, have little or no empathy and even less self-restraint. Self-reflection and collaboration are virtually impossible.

Therefore, it is important to **schedule an ideal time** to discuss this very serious marriage problem. You must choose a time that is convenient and agreeable to both of you, and set the mood for success by creating a loving, positive, even enjoyable environment.

In some cases, I've advised clients to drive through the mountains or book a hotel room and sit in a hot tub together while they talk this out. These are better settings than sitting at the kitchen table and hashing it out. A change of scenery and mood can go a long way.

Before you have this discussion, do a little prep work by reading through the same handful of key strategies in Part III that I mentioned earlier in this section: Day 1 (voice tone); Day 5 (get to the root of arguments); Day 20 (empathy); Day 22 (respect); Day 27 (humility); Day 28 (learn to communicate); and Day 29 (manage intense emotion and anger).

While many other strategies will facilitate this heart-to-heart conversation, these ones are particularly relevant. It is essential that you are able to tell your spouse just how hurtful his or her behavior is to you, how it is destroying the happiness in the home, and how it is chipping away at your loving partnership.

You must be able to have this conversation without hitting a wall of angry defensiveness or having the discussion automatically shift to criticism of you.

Of course, you are partly responsible for the negative dynamics that have been established in your relationship; however, it always takes two to tango and your partner must be willing to look at his or her behavior, too.

It is equally important that your spouse be able to open up and express his or her feelings about his or her behavior. Many people who behave in a belligerent way feel deep regret, shame and humiliation after the fact and do want to change.

If this is the case with your partner, treat his or her vulnerability with care. Show empathy and strive to help him or her understand the root emotions that are triggering the behavior.

This does require a bit of a balancing act: you will have to balance compassion with the strong message that you will not tolerate the behavior any longer. And you have to mean it.

Through it all, remember that the purpose is to work as a team. The goal is to strengthen your partnership by identifying what triggers your partner's behavior (without allowing him or her to blame others for it). You must then work together to manage those triggers in a practical, day to day way.

Brainstorm ways to avoid, reduce or manage the poor behavior...

For some couples, this requires changes in lifestyle such as reducing alcohol intake or looking for a lower-stress job. It may also require the establishment of new "household rules," such as a ban on swearing, name-calling or yelling in the home.

For other couples, this requires finding a way to derail the runaway train of poor behavior as soon as it begins (remember, once the poor behavior has escalated to a certain point, it is virtually impossible to stop). This is a very subjective and couple-specific process.

For example, I had one female client who, whenever her husband began to "lose it," would stand in front of him and lift her shirt to show him her breasts.

As soon as she did this, he would start to laugh and catch himself, quickly realizing how his behavior was spiking and finding perspective in the humor of her actions.

This kind of levity won't work for all couples; however, it does illustrate the kind of stop-it-in-its-tracks approach that is necessary, and how each couple must tailor their approach to their own personalities.

Let's say that you and your spouse have had a good heart-to-heart about the belligerence, defensiveness or criticism in your marriage. You've both committed to changing it and brainstormed ways to avoid or manage it; however, nothing changes. What then?

When enough is enough...

Well, this might be time to do what you should have done from day one: let your feet do the talking and stop tolerating the behavior by leaving the home. A belligerent, defensive or critical spouse sometimes needs that kind of wake-up call.

He or she may need a reminder that people tend to leave the presence of those who yell at, bully or call them names. People tend to walk away from those who constantly criticize them yet rise up in angry defensiveness when asked, even gently asked, to look at their own behavior. A separation may be what it takes to motivate a belligerent partner to pursue professional help, such as anger management or personal counselling.

Another option is to try the Day 7 (take a detour) lifeline in Part III. This strategy can also help you find a way to derail the runaway train of your partner's belligerence, criticism or defensiveness by interrupting this predictable pattern and preventing it from escalating to a crisis point.

If you feel that leaving the home would not help the situation and your partner is unwilling to discuss this issue or change his or her behavior, this strategy may be your best bet.

A final point, here. Sometimes belligerent behavior isn't loud or aggressive. Sometimes it's quite the opposite. Sometimes a spouse wields control in a marriage not by rising up, but by pulling back. He or she may simply fail to engage in discussion or in any efforts to improve the marriage. Basically, he or she is a "no show."

This is the spouse who buys a marriage book, but never reads it. It's the spouse who says he or she will help more around the house, but never does. It's the spouse who says you'll spend the weekend together, but then disappears with friends.

As a result, the other spouse is left in a state of uncertainty and frustration, forever trying to "fill in the blanks" of his or her partner's silence, absence, inaction or chronic passivity.

Again, your best bet when facing this type of behavior is to let your actions speak louder than your words. Stop repeating yourself by expressing the same complaints or questions. We both know your partner isn't listening anymore.

Instead, think about the Day 7 (take a detour) lifeline. The more you can interrupt this predictable pattern, the more your partner will realize that you're done singing the same song.

Part III

One Month to a Happier,

Healthier Marriage

Saving your marriage doesn't have to be a complicated, emotionally-draining or exhaustive process. Simple changes in behavior and outlook, especially when combined with a few essential interpersonal and communication skills, can dramatically improve a couple's relationship and home life.

For those facing more serious marriage problems, incorporating the "crisis care" insight from the previous section can bring a little more insight into these strategies.

I talk a lot about throwing "lifelines" into a marriage. By this, I mean implementing new and more positive behaviors, attitudes, habits and skills into your relationship and home life.

These small changes can lead to big, beautiful changes in a marriage and household.

For example, take the case of a husband who arrives home every evening to find the dog lying on the front mat just inside the door, blocking his entry in the house.

Instantly irritated, he gives the dog a kick or a shove and says, "Get out of my way, you stupid dog!"

His kids – who have seen the whole thing – feel sorry for the dog and run after it, quietly resenting their father's treatment of the family pet.

Mom, making dinner in the kitchen, rolls her eyes at her husband's miserable homecoming.

The evening is off to an unpleasant start and interactions between mom, dad and kids aren't likely to improve much.

Now let's throw a lifeline into this scenario – that is, let's change this pattern of behavior just a little bit to see whether the family dynamics improve.

The husband arrives home in the evening to find the dog lying on the front mat just inside the door, blocking his entry into the house.

Remembering a certain lifeline (in this case Day 17's "Good good-byes and happy hellos"), he swallows his irritation, bends down to scratch the dog's ears and says, "Kids, can you call Fluffy? I don't want to step on him."

It is far more likely that by making this small change to his normal pattern of behavior, this father is going to ignite a positive chain reaction in his household.

The kids are going to be happier to see him. They are going to rush to the door to get the dog out of their dad's way, and likely either initiate or receive a hug from him in the process.

If dad had any lingering traces of irritation, a welcome-home hug from his kids wipes it away.

Mom, noticing the change, greets him with a warm smile.

The evening is off to a great start: this couple and their family are likely to enjoy each other's company in an easygoing, loving manner for the rest of the night.

Some of the lifelines in this section are things you may already know. They are positive behaviors, reactions and ways of communicating that we know result in happier marriages and family lives.

Yet these are the very things that we forget to do over time and need to be reminded of. We need to reignite our mindfulness and we need to reinforce the day-in, day-out behaviors that we know can make or break a marriage and family.

Other lifelines are more substantial and will offer comprehensive strategies for better communication, resolving general and specific conflict, improving interactions, enhancing intimacy between husband and wife, creating a sense of family solidary, encouraging respect and empathy the home and so on.

These types of skills are essential to keep a marriage and family together, and they can be used in conjunction with the "crisis care" material presented earlier.

How to Use Lifelines

Every day, for the next thirty days, you will read a new lifeline and incorporate its strategy, attitude or direction into your marriage and home life.

If you and your spouse are working together, you can each read the day's lifeline; however, these lifelines can also be used by spouses who are working alone to save or improve their marriage.

Because it is essential that you understand the purpose of these lifelines and keep them front-and-center in your mind, I suggest that you read each lifeline three times a day: when you first awake, again at mid-day and then just before you and your spouse reconnect at the end of the day (i.e. just before you and/or your spouse leave work for home).

This will help you stay in the right frame of mind and positive emotional mood required for these lifelines to do their work.

You will see that some lifelines focus on practical things, such as communication skills, resolving conflict, improving interactions, enhancing intimacy and so on.

Others focus on marriage-strengthening concepts from gratitude and appreciation to perspective and devotion.

Still others focus on providing everyone in the family with a voice and having fun.

If you will be using these lifelines alone, without your spouse actively participating, be sure that you don't skip those that you feel are not as important as others, or only commit to them half-heartedly because they don't seem that relevant to you.

A certain strategy or idea may not resonate with you all that much, but it may be end up being the very thing that your spouse or family has been waiting to see in the marriage or home.

For example, let's say I'm having an office consultation with a wife about her marriage problems. I ask, "Do you think your husband feels appreciated?" She quickly replies, "Yes, of course he does. Our problem is that he tries to control every dime I spend."

When I sit down with her husband, however, it's a different story. He admits that, whenever he feels unappreciated for how hard he works for their money, he picks a fight about what she is spending it on.

My point is this: don't assume that your spouse would complain about the same issues, see things the same way as you do or point out the same weak spots in the marriage that you would.

These lifelines cover an expansive cross-section of ideas that can help you avoid any number of relationship problems and heal those ills you have, even if you're not yet completely sure what is causing them. Try everything.

I have laid out these thirty lifelines in an organic order, in an arrangement that I feel flows from one concept to another in a naturally progressive way.

I am confident that you will begin to see positive changes in your marriage and home after the first few days of putting these relationship strategies into use. After a full month, my hope is that your marriage will be on much stronger ground.

That being said, I encourage you to quickly skim through all thirty lifelines before you begin to get the big picture and to see where certain issues or concepts are located.

If you are struggling right now with a certain issue that doesn't appear until day twenty-eight, don't wait for it. Focus on it first and then follow through with the other daily lifelines in the order that you feel best suits your particular situation.

Finally, be sure to go back and review the lifelines you have already used so that you can continue to incorporate them into your marriage and home life.

It is pointless to talk or interact more positively for only a day! The strategies presented here are meant to be cumulative and permanent in your relationship. At least once a week, go back and quickly revisit all of them.

Now get going. And good luck.

30 Lifelines to Save Your Relationship

Day 1
Lifeline: Voice tone.

One of the easiest and most effective ways to create a "happy home" atmosphere is to speak to your spouse and family in a way that builds them up, not tears them down.

On the other hand, one of the most certain ways to create a miserable home environment is to speak to your spouse and family in a negative way.

Indeed, nasty voice tone is one of the most common complaints I hear people make about each other and about the "vibe" in their marriage and household.

The first lifeline I will dispense is this simple but essential task: to improve the voice tone you use when speaking to your spouse and children.

Open your ears and listen to the way your voice sounds to them. Watch out for tones that send a message of criticism, contempt or condescension.

When you hear them, quickly correct yourself by speaking in tones that convey feelings of friendliness, affection, patience and respect.

A positive voice tone has a domino effect in a marriage and in a home. When you speak to your family in warm tones, you increase the feeling of emotional warmth between all family members, including you and your spouse. That leads to kinder words and more loving interactions.

To Do: A picture says a thousand words, right? To reinforce how ugly things can get when you speak to your spouse or kids in a nasty voice tone, I want you to stand in front of the bathroom mirror and look at yourself. Now, speak – out loud – in a nasty voice tone and notice how your expression changes.

Ideally, you should re-enact something you said to your spouse or child using the same contempt, criticism or condescension that you used when you spoke to them.

How do you look? Not very nice, right? Well, that is what your spouse or child is seeing and hearing. And it is extremely damaging to a marriage and the vibe in the household.

Now, change your voice tone. Speak aloud using a warmer, more loving and respectful voice tone.

How do you look? It's a much more attractive picture, isn't it? Make a mental note of what your family is seeing when you speak in pleasant versus unpleasant voice tones. Note how your expression changes, how your eyes either glow or glare, how your body posture is either open or closed.

What do you want your spouse and children to see when they look at you?

Day 2
Lifeline: Listen to your spouse.

"You never listen to me!"

"What?"

It's the oldest joke in the book. But it isn't very funny when a spouse routinely feels unheard or ignored by his or her spouse.

Why do we stop listening to each other? Well, sometimes we're distracted: work, worries, technology, feeling unwell, or being in a strong emotional mood (good or bad) can all preoccupy us and make us poor listeners. It happens, and often it's as innocent as it is unavoidable.

But sometimes we stop listening to what our spouse has to say because we stop caring what our spouse has to say. This lack of caring doesn't need to be callous, although it can be. In cases of serious marital troubles, a spouse acts from a place of resentment, frustration or even contempt. They interpret anything their partner says as annoying and stupid.

Most of the time, however, we stop listening because we simply stop hearing. We grow so accustomed to our spouse's voice and presence that we start "tuning it out." We don't mean to, it just happens.

But this innocence doesn't excuse the behavior or make it any less irritating or insulting to our partner. A spouse who feels unheard also feels unimportant and unloved.

Today's lifeline is on listening to your spouse. This doesn't just mean absently nodding your head and being able to parrot the last three words of what your partner said. It means *active* listening.

Keeping eye contact, staying attentive and being fully present when your partner speaks. It means putting down your phone, closing your laptop and looking at your partner – not the television – when he or she is speaking.

Show emotion and interest when your partner is speaking.

Empathize with your spouse's feelings, whether he or she is frustrated or worried, happy or excited. Show interest in what your partner has to say.

What if you aren't interested in it, you ask? Get interested, if for no other reason than to please your spouse. He or she will notice the effort and will likely begin to show more interest in what you have to say.

If you really can't get interested in what your partner is talking about – let's say a hobby or drawn-out work drama – fall back on basic manners. It is impolite to shrug off what another person has to say, especially when that person is the most important person in your entire life.

Of special importance, be sure to focus on listening to your partner's opinions, preferences or even complaints about your lifestyle or relationship. I have had many clients say to me, "I had no idea my wife/husband was unhappy! This divorce came out of nowhere!"

Yet when questioned, the client can recall many times his or her partner expressed dissatisfaction: a lack of help with housework, a loss of sexual intimacy, feeling ignored or disrespected and so on. Open your ears – and your mind and heart – to what your spouse has to say.

In the same way, focus on listening to what your kids are trying to tell you. They might talk a lot or never say a word – either way, they have their own style of communicating and you as a parent need to figure that out.

When your children talk to you, stop what you're doing and give them your full attention. Today more than ever, we as parents need to be vigilant to the things our children are trying to tell us.

Day 3
Lifeline: Cheerfulness.

Don't worry, I'm not talking about walking around with a vacant smile and acting like you're in a drug-induced stupor of constant bliss. I'm talking about choosing to have a cheerful disposition as much as possible rather than succumbing to snarkiness and negativity.

People are like magnets. On one end, we have the power to attract people to us. We do this by having a cheerful nature that naturally draws others – most importantly our spouse – toward us.

On the other end, we have the power to repel people – most importantly our spouse and family members– away from us. We do this by being cheerless. By being negative, humorless and generally unpleasant to be around.

To Do: Act like the sunny side of a magnet by having a cheerful disposition. Offer your partner and kids a smile, not a scowl.

Instead of whining about what went wrong in your day, talk about what went right. Rather than criticizing someone (family member, friend or even a stranger) find something nice to say about that person.

Day 4

Lifeline: Physical & emotional affection.

In the early phase of a relationship, we can't keep our hands off each other. The idea of going to work all day and not being able to embrace, kiss or caress our beloved is torture! We crave to be close to them and to have that kind of affectionate contact.

Fast-forward a few years, and many spouses say they go days without really touching each other. Deep, passionate kisses become quick pecks on the cheek. Long, tight embraces become a quick pat on the shoulder.

This lifeline is about finding that happy medium between lustful affection and lasting affection. It is on increasing the amount of times that you and your partner touch every day: humans respond emotionally to touch, so use that to your advantage.

It is also about enhancing emotional affection. You know that "warm fuzzy" feeling you get when someone makes you feel loved or adored? Give that feeling to your spouse on a daily basis.

To Do: Rub your spouse's back or run your fingers through his or her hair. Make your kisses longer and deeper, and your embraces more loving and intimate. Give your partner a sensual massage in bed, preferably a full-body massage that lasts at least thirty minutes. Make sure that you use a good-quality massage oil or lotion to enhance the experience.

Day 5
Lifeline: Get to the root of arguments.

You know what it means to "get to the root" of a problem. It means recognizing that the real reason for a conflict is often hidden below the surface of our words and interactions. This lifeline uses this kind of tree metaphor to illustrate the way that couples often argue. Stay with me – it'll make sense in a moment.

Picture a large tree. It has hundreds of branches and thousands of leaves. When the storm winds blow, the branches and leaves wave around like mad. They make a lot of noise and, if the wind blows hard enough, they can even break off and scatter around to make a big mess.

Yet the roots – which are fewer in number than the branches and leaves – remain stuck in the ground, deep and hidden. In all the noise and fury of the storm winds, the roots are all but forgotten. They're there, but the loud, messy branches and leaves put on such a show that we don't even think about the roots.

Relationship conflict can be like that. Every argument, every eye-roll, every angry word or snide comment, every fight about the same thing over and over again, is a branch or a leaf on the tree. There are thousands of these individual leaves, little battles that chip away at our marriage. They blow back and forth in the winds of anger, resentment or misunderstanding, making noise and making a mess.

Meanwhile, the real reason for the argument is hidden below the ground. That's the root of the problem, although we seldom have the patience or insight to dig up the root and see why it's rotten. Instead, we stay at the top of the tree, having arguments about trivial things, and ripping up branches to throw at each other.

Today, I want you to stop focusing on "top of the tree" arguments – all those little spats and nasty interactions that represent the thousand leaves – and start focusing on the underlying "root" of the argument or problem.

You will find that there are fewer roots than leaves. Why? Because one "root cause" of conflict – such as feeling unappreciated or unheard – can lead to countless fights and arguments that may appear to be unrelated, but are in fact all rooted in a feeling of not being appreciated or heard. The following exercise can help you climb down the tree, and get to the root of your issues.

To Do: The "argument tree" exercise.

1. Draw a tree. It should have a trunk with three to five roots extending out below it, and ten to fifteen branches extending above it in all directions (draw the branches and roots as simple straight lines that you will be able to write on).

2. Along each branch, write down as many arguments or fights that you can think of. Be as specific as you can. For example, you might write "when he forgot about my birthday" or "when she returned my car to me with an empty fuel tank" or "when we had a fight at the restaurant about how much the bill was" or "when he said I was putting on weight."

3. Next, think back to that grade-school exercise where you grouped similar things together. When you look at the arguments at the top of the tree, do some of them have common roots? That is, are some of these arguments triggered by the same emotion or emotions? These triggering emotions might include feeling unappreciated, fearful, unheard, unloved, criticized, abandoned, disrespected or stressed out.

4. Along each root, write down the main emotion(s) that tend to trigger arguments.

5. When you next find yourself arguing with your spouse, try to focus on these root emotions and talk about them. You might say, "I feel fearful that you're falling out of love with me" or "I think we're both feeling unappreciated" or "We need to make a good budget because I am stressed out about money."

When you approach your arguments with some depth of understanding – rather than just having a superficial fight about any number of trivial things – you have a far better chance of working together to resolve a problem. You are more likely to focus on the issue rather than just complain about each other or re-enact past fights.

As importantly, focusing on the root(s) of your arguments changes the dynamics of your conflict style. That is, it changes the way you fight and interrupts the habitual, here-we-go-again futility of your endless parade of petty arguments.

This can allow you to see and tackle problems in a new and different way, rather than just having the same argument – sometimes using the exact same words! – again and again.

An example might help put this exercise into context. Consider a wife who constantly "nags" her husband for a number of trivial things.

Along the branches at the top of the tree, she might write things like, "he leaves crumbs on the counter" and "he folds the towels the wrong way" and "he lets the kids stay up past their bedtime" and "he leaves me home while he goes out to have a drink with his co-workers."

She seems like a control freak, doesn't she? And you can imagine that their home life isn't very relaxed or happy.

Yet once this wife starts to focus on the root emotion that triggers these (seemingly) unrelated arguments, she realizes that there is a common emotional denominator – she is feeling overwhelmed.

Whenever she nags her husband – whether it's about housework or parenting or socializing – she is driven by a sense of being overwhelmed by everything she has on her plate.

It isn't that she minds the crumbs or the occasional late bedtime. She doesn't really care how the towels are folded and she actually supports her husband socializing with his co-workers. But when she feels overwhelmed, she snaps at him over anything and everything.

Now, instead of arguing about the crumbs and the towels and the kids' bedtime and so on, she and her husband can climb down out of the tree and focus on the root issue – the fact that she is feeling overwhelmed.

Even better, they can now begin to brainstorm solutions to the problem. How can they re-arrange their schedules or lifestyles so that she feels less stressed and more supported on a daily basis?

Once that happens, she is far more likely to let the little things slide and to be a happier, more relaxed spouse. Her husband can stop walking on eggshells around her, and their marriage can grow stronger.

Day 6
Lifeline: Praise your partner.

I have previously talked about the fact that people are like magnets. On one end, we have the power to attract others to us. On the other end, we have the ability to repel them away from us. I want you to keep that mind for this lifeline.

Spouses stay with partners who make them feel good about themselves. They stay with partners who focus on their positive traits, not obsess about their flaws. After all, nobody's perfect.

Today, I want you to think like a magnet. Every chance you get, I want you to praise your partner. Flatter his or her appearance, accomplishments, personality and character. Don't make it gushing or fake – keep it sincere and simple.

I especially want you to focus on flattering your partner when you're around other people. Speak highly of your partner in front of family, friends and especially your children, as this is incredibly meaningful to a spouse. This tells your spouse that, "I have your back. I'm your greatest advocate." It also fosters a sense of solidarity, partnership and appreciation in a marriage.

Do the same thing with your children. Sing their praises when you are around family and friends, and be sure they hear you and your spouse talking about what great kids you have.

Day 7
Lifeline: Take a detour.

Today's lifeline offers an easy way to knock the wind out of those nasty, pointless little arguments that couples often find become a habit in the marriage. In fact, this simple strategy can be used when a couple finds themselves falling into almost any kind of predictable behavioral pattern, whether it's conflict, the daily routine or just plain boredom.

Let me ask you this: What do you do if you're driving along a road and you realize it's heading to the same negative, nowhere town you've been before? Well, you stop the car and head in a different direction. You take a detour, even if it takes you off-road.

In fact, it doesn't matter where the detour takes you – as long as you don't head back to that negative, nowhere town. You already know what's there – conflict, apathy, boredom. So you might as well take your chances by taking a different route, even one that you haven't travelled before. At the very least, you won't end up in the same dead-end town.

And that in itself is progress. Why? Because in my experience, many couples grow distant and get divorced because of a sense of hopelessness. A sense that nothing will ever change. A sense that they just keep hitting the same dead-end over and over again.

To combat this sense of "nothing will ever change," I want you to spend today thinking about the predictable behavioral patterns that you and your partner fall into, and that you feel are chipping away at your relationship.

Be on high-alert for those patterns. When you feel yourself falling into one, stop in your tracks. Stop whatever you're doing or saying and start doing and saying something different. Take a detour. The idea is to stop the cycle, to break the habit, to take a different path. Any path, as long as it isn't the same negative, go-nowhere path you normally take.

For example, take the case of a couple who has the same fight almost every day after supper.

The moment they are finished eating, the wife stands up and says, "Let's clean off the table." The husband rolls his eyes, rubs his stomach and says, "Oh come on, let's relax and watch a little television first…it'll wait." The wife lets out an exasperated sigh. "You know I can't relax until the table is cleaned off!"

At that, the husband starts grabbing things off the table and, in an obviously irritated mood, shoves plates and glasses into the dishwasher. His wife, also now irritated, sighs again and reorganizes the dishwasher. "The dishes won't come clean if you load them like that," she gripes. "How many times do I have to tell you the same thing?"

You can guess how the rest of this couple's evening is going to go.

Now let's see how this couple might take a detour to avoid the same negative, nowhere dead-end argument.

The moment they are finished eating, the wife stands up and says, "Let's clean off the table." The husband rolls his eyes, rubs his stomach and says, "Oh come on, let's relax and watch a little television first…it'll wait."

The wife thinks "detour." Instead of falling into the habitual argument they always have, she recognizes the pattern developing and she stops in her tracks. By sheer force of will, she smiles and says, "You're right. Let's go snuggle on the couch for a while. I missed you today."

Not only has her detour steered them clear of their usual argument, but her unexpected behavior has caught her husband's attention – and in a very good way.

He knows that she likes to clean off the table before relaxing, so her agreement to watch some television first means a lot to him. He knows it isn't easy for her and that she is doing it to avoid the argument.

Now, the evening is far more likely to be an enjoyable one. The husband may change his mind and say, "That is very sweet of you...but let's clear the table now so you can relax." That is, he may try to return the favor. Or perhaps they will just snuggle on the couch and enjoy being close.

Either way, the wife has cancelled their regularly-scheduled 6:43 pm argument.

Day 8
Lifeline: Power down & log out.

The obsessive use and over-use of technology – smartphones, texting, social media, Internet surfing and so forth – is taking a heavy toll on marriages.

It is extremely irritating to try and have a conversation with one's partner when that partner is staring at his or her phone or computer, perhaps even carrying on a conversation with someone else via texting or social media.

When spouses choose to spend time on an electronic device rather than with their spouse, they send a definite message to that spouse: "This gadget is more interesting and more important to me than you are. Whoever I'm texting or chatting with on this gadget is more interesting and important to me than you are."

Today's lifeline is to stop or at least seriously limit your unnecessary and social use of technology. Log out. Power down. Do not text anyone else in your partner's presence. Stop posting updates on social media. Do not bring your smartphone or tablet into the bedroom.

When you stop looking at your gadgets and start looking into your partner's eyes, you make a powerful statement. "You're the most important and interesting person in my life."

It's time to put technology in its place. Update your relationship instead of updating your software. Reconnect with your spouse instead of reading junk email. Reignite your passionate partnership instead of powering-up your laptop.

To Do: Let your partner see that you are taking real steps to limit the use of technology – particularly texting, protracted Internet surfing and social media – in your household. Suggest that you start leaving your smartphones in another room instead of sleeping with them on the nightstand.

Also, suggest that you come up with a few "tech rules" together, such as not answering or checking the phone during mealtimes or movie nights unless it is absolutely necessary.

Lead by example: let your kids know that staying connected to family is more important than staying connected to technology. At the same time, don't just tell them to "put down the phone" and then ignore them. Fill in the time with some family fun.

Day 9
Lifeline: Show desire.

Sexual desire is a powerful emotion. When we feel it, it's hard to focus on anything other than the object of our desire. He or she is all we can think about, fantasize about. Nothing else seems important. Our every waking moment is spent thinking of ways to get close to him or her again. And soon!

It is equally thrilling to feel like we are the object of someone else's desire. In fact, many partners who have had an emotional or physical affair will say that it was the *feeling* of being desired by their forbidden paramour that proved irresistible, not the paramour herself or himself. People often have affairs because of the way the other person makes them feel.

Today (and especially tonight), I want you to focus on making your partner feel as though he or she is the object of your burning sexual desire.

Let him or her experience the thrill of feeling desired in a sexual way. Send a sexual text. Come home with flowers. Whisper a sexy sweet nothing into his or her ear. Let your spouse see your eyes wandering over his or her body. Tell your spouse that you've been fantasizing about him or her all day. Flatter your spouse's appearance and let him or her know that you can't wait until bedtime.

Not only will this lifeline boost your spouse's ego, it will likely increase his or her desire for you, too. And when spouses desire each other, they don't notice anyone else.

Day 10
Lifeline: Memory lane.

People love to talk about themselves. I don't mean in a self-absorbed way, I just mean they love to feel that someone is interested in them and what they have to contribute.

They like to share their experiences and especially their memories. It gives them an opportunity to relive a time or revisit a place that held great meaning to them. People particularly love to share their past memories with those who are important to them, like a spouse.

Today, you will walk down memory lane with your spouse in two distinct ways.

First, you will focus on your spouse's personal memory lane. You will show genuine interest and curiosity about your partner's past, including where he or she grew up, lived, went to school, played and so on.

Where did your spouse go on holidays as a child? What does your spouse remember most about being a child? In what neighborhood did your spouse used to ride his or her bike or run around the playground with friends? Where did your spouse used to go for ice-cream as kid? You get the idea.

Second, you will focus on your marriage's memory lane. When was the last time you talked about the day you met, your honeymoon or the time you stumbled upon that amazing café in New Orleans?

When was the last time you thought about the first house you bought together or the hilarious water fight you had with your kids a few summers back?

You have an amazing inventory of experiences as a couple. This inventory binds you together and gives you a shared history that you need to revisit occasionally so that it doesn't become lost to time.

To bring greater emotional impact to these walks down memory lane, add a visual dimension to the experience by using Google Earth to revisit first the places where your spouse grew up – his or her home town, childhood homes or playgrounds, family vacation spots, etc. – and then the places where you and your spouse have lived or travelled to as a couple.

Using street view, zoom in on the streets your spouse rode his or her bicycle on as a child. Walk up to the doors of his or her childhood home or school. Drive down the streets where he or she used to travel with his or her parents.

Visit the cabin on the lake where he or she spent summer vacations with loving grandparents, catching frogs on the dock or feeding ducks on the shore.

Don't rush these journeys. Let your partner enjoy the nostalgia and tell you about the people and places he or she hasn't thought about in decades.

Next, use street view to zoom in on the streets you and your spouse have travelled on together.

The houses you've lived in. The park in which you were married. The beach where you had your honeymoon. The hospital where your child was born. The art gallery in New York City or the farmer's market on Salt Spring Island where you found that stunning painting, the one that now hangs in your living room.

You can let your kids share in this experience by showing them where their parents grew up, met, honeymooned and so on. You can also show them the hospital where they were born and any other towns or homes you lived in as a family. Kids love to have a sense of where they came from.

Day 11
Lifeline: Live in the moment.

Couples are often overly focused on the future. They might think or say that life will be better "when we buy a new house," or "when I have a new job" or "when we're out of debt" or "when we have a baby" or "when the kids are older." There's this idea that happiness is just over the horizon, that tomorrow will bring more happiness, more fulfillment, more money, more whatever.

But what about today?

When we are overly focused on tomorrow, we squander the thousand beautiful moments that today has to offer. The morning cup of coffee we share with our spouse. The inside joke. The taste of food or wine on our lips. The flirtatious wink or loving embrace. The movie nights cuddled on the couch. The moonlight walk. The pillow talk.

I find that people don't always remember the "big things" like expensive vacations or new houses. Often, they remember the "little things." Those little routines of good-night kisses and morning smiles, and everything in between. Yet too often we don't appreciate them.

To Do: Slow down and live in the moment. When you feel your thoughts drifting into the future, pull them back to the present. Focus on making the most of today with your spouse and family.

Day 12
Lifeline: Meal-time makeover.

We live busy lives nowadays. As often as not, "meal time" means eating a drive-thru cheeseburger in the car or chowing down on a pizza in front of the television.

This doesn't just result in indigestion and unhealthy eating habits. It also results in a disconnection between spouses and families as they neglect one of the most fundamental bonding rituals of domestic life – sharing meals together at the kitchen or dining room table.

Today, you will focus on slowing down and creating more meaningful meal-time habits as a couple and family. Sit at the table to enjoy good food and even better company over the supper hour.

This is the ideal time to unwind from your respective days and reconnect. At a minimum, you and your spouse and family should be eating together at the table at least three or four times weekly.

Although suppertime is usually the most relaxing time to be in each other's company, don't give up if you can't make that work. Sharing regular breakfasts or occasional lunches together can also work.

Even if spouses are both at work, they can eat at the same time in each other's virtual presence via Skype or other live-video services.

Make it a habit to only discuss pleasant, high-interest topics at the dinner table. It is not the place to argue or worry about how much you owe in taxes or rag on the kids for something they did wrong. Meal-time is a time to nourish the body and the spirit. It is also a time to nourish your bond as husband, wife and family.

To Do: Give your kitchen or dining room table a makeover so that it is more enjoyable to sit at. Put on a new tablecloth or purchase new dinnerware and silverware to add an elegant and novel dimension to meal-time.

Lower the lights and, if you like, play some soft classical music – or your kids' favorite music! – in the background. Light a few candles at the table.

If you have pre-teen or teen-aged children, take their lead when it comes to conversation. I have heard many parents complain that their kids never talk to them; however, it sometimes happens that parents inadvertently shut-down their kids by dismissing as boring or unimportant those topics that their kids want to talk about.

When your children grow up and move out, you and your spouse will have more than enough quiet meal-times to talk about the things that interest you. Listen to your kids while you can. Those little voices are getting bigger every year.

Day 13
Lifeline: Show appreciation.

Of all the complaints I have heard from unhappy spouses over the years, "I don't feel appreciated" is either at or near the top of the list. Even if couples are going through a pressing crisis like infidelity, the talk often shifts from an acute feeling of broken trust to a chronic feeling of being unappreciated.

Just like a runny nose is a universal symptom of a cold, feeling unappreciated is a universal symptom of an unhappy marriage.

And just as you can avoid a cold with regular handwashing (and a little bit of luck), so too can you avoid feelings of being unappreciated with regular words and gestures of appreciation.

Unhappy spouses will often ask me, "Why should I appreciate my spouse when he/she doesn't appreciate me?" My answer is, "Because you married this person and it's the right thing to do…and because your partner is far more likely to appreciate *you* if he or she feels appreciated *by you*."

Without a doubt, the best and most loving way to motivate your spouse to appreciate you more is to focus on appreciating him or her more.

Today's lifeline is to speak words of appreciation to your spouse. This doesn't just mean saying "thank you" more. It means noticing everything your partner does – the big things and the little things – that contribute to making your life and marriage better, and expressing sincere appreciation for those things.

Don't forget to perform gestures of appreciation, too. Make a spouse's favorite meal or order-in to give him or her a break from cooking. Help more around the house. Give your spouse the quiet time he or she needs to finish those work files or just power-down from a long, busy day. Draw your spouse a bath. Buy a book you know your partner would like, and then order him or her to bed early to relax and read.

If you have kids, praise your spouse in front of your children, so that he or she knows your children are growing up with appreciative spirits.

When your kids do something nice (for you or for someone else), express your appreciation for them, too. We all long for that sense of acknowledgement, no matter our age.

Day 14
Lifeline: Face your fears.

Much marital conflict and unhappiness is unknowingly fear-driven. For example, a spouse who comes across as a "control freak" about money may in fact be fearful about the household debt load. He or she may not be a controlling personality at all, but rather afraid of the consequences of a partner's overspending or failure to remain on budget.

Parenting is another example. A parent who comes across as too inflexible may be fearful of raising unruly children who will not succeed in life.

At the same time, a parent who comes across excessively lenient may be fearful of driving a moody teenager out of the home.

Even a spouse who comes across as unfeeling or judgmental may in fact be feeling fear. A spouse who points out how much weight his or her partner has gained, or who criticizes a partner's lifestyle may not be a total jerk.

He or she may actually be fearful that a partner's health or interest in life is declining, and worried about what that means for the marriage and their future.

When we understand what scares us – and what scares our spouse – we are able to focus our energy and conversation on the root emotion or problem rather than arguing about those nasty, pointless "top of the tree" things: refer back to Day 5 (get to the root of arguments).

Today's lifeline strategy is to tap into your fears. Are you worried about money? Are you concerned about your or your partner's health or lifestyle choices? Do you have concerns about the relationship you have with your kids? Are you afraid of growing older or becoming less attractive to your partner?

Tap into your partner's fears, too, and do your best to address and soothe them. If your partner isn't ready to talk about his or her fears, don't press the matter.

Try to figure it out on your own. After all, you know your partner best and there is a good chance he or she has expressed certain concerns or worries in the past. Even if he or she hasn't, do some thinking and try to come up with a few best guesses.

Partners who are able to safely express their fears – and who have the motivation and focus to make changes that will alleviate those fears – will enjoy a profoundly stronger and happier marriage than those who lack these abilities. They will also have far fewer misunderstandings and feelings of resentment.

Day 15
Lifeline: Gratitude.

Many of us have a "thankless" streak. We might be having a lovely day, one that runneth over with wonderful moments with family, friends and colleagues – and yet the moment that even the smallest of annoyances crops up, our mood turns sour and irritable. Give us a thousand happy times and a single unhappy one, and we'll focus on the unhappy one. Sheesh.

Unfortunately, many of us bring this attitude of thanklessness into our marriage and home. Instead of feeling gratitude for our spouse and giving thanks to the universe for all that we have, we dwell on what we interpret as imperfections in our life.

Not only does this make us a negative person to live with, it unnecessarily robs us of a thousand opportunities for joy.

Unless you can accept the perfection of your life as it is today, you will never be able to have a grateful heart.

Gratitude is a life-changing choice. It is also an emotion, to be sure, but first and foremost it's a choice. It's a lifestyle decision, a personal "default setting" that makes us fall on the sunny-side up as much as possible. It's a good habit, not a bad one.

Today, strive to stay focused on a feeling of gratitude for all that you have in your life. Wrap yourself in it. Breathe it in. Remember that gratitude for one's spouse and family is a choice that only you can make.

Day 16
Lifeline: Fun and laughter.

The couple that plays together stays together. I truly believe that. There have been times in my marriage and family life when I've thought, "Wow, I can't remember the last time I heard Don laugh." I now make the effort to make him laugh every day and, wow, what a difference. It's as though our home gets visibly brighter and tangibly happier.

Today's lifeline strategy is to strive for a "funnier" marriage and home life, one that makes you, your partner and your children smile and laugh every day. Never underestimate the bonding and healing power of humor. It feels good to laugh. It fills the body with endorphins and makes people want to be around each other.

Don't you feel better in the company of some people than others? Aren't there people in your life that you enjoy because they always have something positive and amusing to say? Be that person for your spouse and kids.

To Do: Make a conscious effort to make your partner and children smile and laugh at least two or three times today and every day. It doesn't matter how you do this. You can tell jokes, have a "most embarrassing moment" family challenge, watch hilarious kitten videos online or rent a comedy. Just make sure the laughter flows freely and that it is good-natured.

At the same time, be sure to laugh when your spouse or kids tell you something funny. It feels good to know that we have made another person laugh. It builds us up. Be the person that makes your family feel this way.

Day 17
Lifeline: Good good-byes & happy hellos.

I often tell my clients about my "60 seconds" theory.

It goes like this: there are sixty seconds in your day that are absolutely pivotal in terms of how you and your spouse will relate to each other for the entire day and night.

These sixty seconds happen in two intervals.

The first interval is the thirty seconds when you and your spouse say your morning "good-byes" as both or one of you leaves the house to go to work for the day.

The second interval is the thirty seconds when you and your spouse say your late-afternoon or evening "hellos" as both or one of you arrives back home at the end of the day.

The tone you set during these brief good-byes and hellos has a profound, lasting effect on how you and your partner will think about each other and interact with each other.

For example, a wife who says good-bye to her husband as he leaves for work by embracing him, telling him to have a good day or remembering to wish him luck – whether it's for a work presentation or a dentist appointment – will have a husband who leaves the home with a smile on his face and feeling of love in his heart.

A wife who welcomes her husband home at the end of the day by meeting him at the door with a smile and a kiss, who remembers to ask how his work presentation or dentist appointment went, and who lets him know that he was truly missed, will have a husband who enters the home with a smile on his face and a feeling of love in his heart.

The feeling is only enhanced if she encourages his children to stop what they are doing and also meet Dad at the door.

Contrast that with what happens in many homes, where spouses leave the house without even bothering to say good-bye to each other.

Spouses who come home at the end of a long, hard day to a house where no one comes to meet them at the door or even seems to notice – or care – that they are home.

What house and spouse would you rather come home to?

Those sixty seconds, that one collective minute of your time, can determine on a daily basis whether your marriage thrives or dives.

That one minute of time can determine whether you and your spouse think happy, positive, loving thoughts about each other all day, or whether you have negative or apathetic thoughts about each other.

It will determine whether you and your spouse look forward to seeing each other all day or whether you dread going home. It will determine whether your evening is spent in laughter, good humor and happy companionship, or in bitterness and indifference.

Today's lifeline is to focus on those all-important good-byes and hellos. It is to part with your spouse in a loving way, and to welcome him or her home with a grateful heart.

Day 18

Lifeline: Your spouse's unmet needs.

Quite often, couples and families fall into what I call fact-based arguments. That is, their disagreements go something like this telephone conversation between an angry wife and husband:

"You said you'd meet me here at the restaurant at five o'clock! I've been sitting here for an hour…where are you?!"

"No, I said I'd be there just after six o'clock. I had to work late tonight, remember?"

"You said you had to work late tomorrow night, not tonight!"

"No, I said it was tonight. I distinctly remember telling you this morning. I handed you your travel mug as you were leaving, and said I had to stay an extra hour."

"I didn't have a travel mug this morning."

"Yes you did. I gave you that blue one."

"I threw that blue travel mug out last week because it leaks. So you couldn't have given it to me this morning."

"Well, I remember giving you one."

"What color was it?"

I could go on…and on…and on. And unfortunately, many people do. These kinds of fact-based arguments aren't just pointless and immeasurably frustrating, they are also destructive to relationships.

People fall into other kinds of destructive conflict patterns, too. They may play the "blame game" where any complaint on another person's part – even a legitimate one – is met with defensiveness and an attempt to avoid accountability by shifting blame onto the other person. In the worst cases, people will even find a way to blame their own poor behavior on someone else.

"I only yell because you don't listen to me!"

It may be true that the other person doesn't listen; however, yelling isn't likely to improve the situation.

The "withdraw and pursue" dance is another destructive style of conflict which is particularly common in marriages. A couple finds themselves arguing and, when things start to heat up, one spouse withdraws by either shutting down or even leaving the home.

This causes the other spouse to pursue him or her by insisting that the conversation or argument carry on until resolution. The pursuing spouse may literally follow or chase his or her spouse around or out of the house.

Do any of these conflict styles or habits look familiar to you? Whether they do or don't, today's lifeline strategy is on trying to understand and fulfill your spouse's "unmet needs" in the relationship, particularly during arguments or times of conflict.

Much of the time, arguments stem from what a person is *not* getting or feeling.

For example, a spouse who waits an hour at a restaurant for his or her partner has an unmet need – to feel prioritized and important.

A child who blames a parent for not listening has an unmet need – to feel heard and validated.

A spouse who pursues a partner around the house, desperate to resolve the conflict, has an unmet need – to feel reassured and loved.

To Do: Today and from now on, keep an eye open for those typical but pointlessly destructive conflict habits, such as fact-based arguments, the blame game and the withdrawal-pursuit dance. Most marriages will have at least trace amounts of these habits and it's always a good idea to wipe them out altogether.

Instead of falling into these or other dead-end, destructive argument styles, try taking a different approach to conflict.

Whenever you find yourself falling into conflict – major or minor – ask yourself this question: "What is my spouse's 'unmet need' right now?"

That is, what is your spouse *not* getting or feeling? Reassurance? Acknowledgement? Love? Respect? A sense of being heard or prioritized?

When you know (or think you know) the answer, do your best to meet or fulfill that need.

Reassure your spouse that you love him or her. You may be arguing, but you are completely committed to the marriage.

Listen to your spouse – *really* listen – so that he or she feels heard, understood and loved. Learn to recognize, understand and fulfill your spouse's unmet needs in the relationship.

This is a very effective way to avoid and resolve conflict, and to approach your problems or arguments from a different angle.

Day 19

Lifeline: Trust & transparency.

It's something I hear spouses say to each other all the time: "You should trust me!"

Yes, spouses should trust each other. But trust doesn't just happen. It isn't a "given."

Like the emotion of love, the emotion of trust develops, slowly but surely, over the months and years of a relationship. And it doesn't just develop out of nothing. It develops as a result of the repeated trustworthy behaviors of each partner.

For that reason, couples need to have specific behaviors – relationship rules, if you will – that nourish feelings of trust.

The most important behavior is transparency. As a rule, couples who wish to foster a spirit of total trust in their marriage should be completely open and transparent with regard to passwords (for phones, computers, email accounts and so on) as well as their whereabouts and their communications with friends, particularly opposite-sex friends or co-workers.

Today's lifeline is about trust and transparency. You've heard the expression, "Those who have nothing to hide, hide nothing." It is absolutely true.

Some partners will claim that passwords and such are private; however, this kind of privacy can only stir feelings of suspicion and insecurity between partners.

This is especially so when a relationship is going through a rough patch, as almost all relationships do now and then. Sometimes privacy can turn into a front for secrecy. And that is antithetical to the very concept of marriage.

To Do: Have an easygoing, non-confrontational discussion with your spouse about trust and transparency in your marriage.

Even if you are not struggling with trust issues right now, you need to have this conversation – in fact, it is far better to have this conversation in advance, before trust is broken, than to wait until the damage is done, emotions are high or wild speculation is running amok.

Ask yourselves: Do you have relationship rules in place that nourish a spirit of trust and trustworthiness in your marriage? Do you and your spouse know each other passwords? Are you open, honest and forthcoming about your whereabouts and the people with whom you're spending your time?

Day 20
Lifeline: Empathy.

There's a difference between sympathy and empathy, and it's an important one to recognize within a marriage and home. A wife might feel sympathy for her husband who is passed over for a major job promotion, one he had been working very hard to receive. She will express her sadness and offer support. Maybe she will make his favorite supper and be extra sweet to him. She loves him and she doesn't want to see him unhappy.

Empathy is different. A wife feels empathy for her husband's lost job opportunity when she herself has experienced a lost job opportunity. She's been there. She has felt the same emotions of disappointment, anger and betrayal. She knows her husband is walking around with a sick feeling in the pit of his stomach because she's had the exact same feeling. She is able to put herself in his place.

Sympathy and empathy are both noble emotions. They show concern, compassion and human warmth. One is not necessarily better than the other.

Nonetheless, empathy may be the more useful of the two emotions to strive for within a marriage. Why? Because being able to feel what your partner feels – or at least trying your very best to do so – lends insight and authenticity to your interactions.

Empathetic ability and insight is even more important when we are dealing with our children. Why? Because kids – particularly pre-teens and teens – are notoriously difficult to communicate with. Asking a teenager, "What's wrong with you?" is going to get you no feedback other than a snide, "Nothing" and a shoulder shrug.

If you can "best guess" a reason for your teen's change in mood, however, you might stand a chance. Saying to a teen, "I know final exams are next week. Are you feeling prepared or do you need some extra help?" is likely to get a more meaningful response than a generic, "What's wrong with you?"

Today's lifeline is about seeing things from the point of view of your spouse and/or children. It is also about feeling the emotions you imagine they might be feeling.

Not only will you learn more about your partner and kids, you will come across as more patient, loving, selfless and understanding to them. This will strengthen your bond as a couple and family unit.

In my capacity as a couples and family mediator, I used to ask my clients – that is, couples and their children – to perform a very simple two-part exercise that I called The Exchange.

This exercise is designed to increase empathetic ability in the home by asking each family member to see and feel an issue from the point of view of other family members.

For a family-focused example, let's say David, a twelve-year-old boy, is starting to misbehave every night before bed.

Bedtime has become the most dreaded time in the day, with mom and dad repeatedly shouting at him to get ready for bed and David slamming doors and drawing out the process as long as possible until everyone in the home is in a foul mood. Despite his misbehavior at home, David is continuing to behave like a perfect angel at school and elsewhere.

Out of desperation – and exhaustion – David's parents have really started to bring down the hammer. Their strategy is to meet his resistance with even greater force and insistence: their voices get louder, they threaten to take away his video game or computer privileges, and even tell him he's "close to a spanking."

The Exchange Part I:
The "Eyeball Exchange"

At this point, I ask David's parents to perform part one of The Exchange: this is the "eyeball exchange" portion of the exercise.

I ask them to see the world through David's eyes.

What is going on in his day? What is happening in the hours before bedtime? What is he seeing happen around him?

Upon reflection, the parents "see" that David's day is actually as busy as theirs is. He has school from 8:30 am until 3:30 pm, and then he is off to soccer practice until 5:00 pm. For supper, they often pick up fast-food and eat in the car on the way home, or eat in front of the television.

Most nights, the family then runs out again for David's sister's dance class. They get home around 7:30 pm, at which time David does a half-hour to an hour of homework. After that, he is told to do his chores. The moment his chores are finished, he is told to get ready for bed.

It doesn't take a parenting expert to see what's going on here – it just takes a parent who has the patience and ability to see the situation from his or her child's point of view.

The Exchange Part II:
The "Emotion Exchange"

I then ask the parents to perform part two of The Exchange: this is the "emotion exchange" portion of the exercise.

I ask them to feel what David must be feeling.

Upon reflection, the parents suspect that David is feeling the stressful fallout of a busy schedule and a lack of "kid time" to play. He may also be lacking quality family time and one-on-one time with each parent, which is making him feel unimportant.

As bedtime nears, his feelings of being "ignored" by his parents all day turn into resentment, and he misbehaves – not out of malice but, quite honestly, out of sadness. His acting out is a cry for the time and affection of his parents.

The Exchange exercise works in the other direction, too – from child to parent. When David is asked to see and feel the situation from the point of view of his parents, he comes to see how his bedtime drama looks like mere misbehavior.

He knows his parents work hard all day and feel very tired at bedtime, so he can empathize with their frustration at bedtime, too.

This kind of exercise not only helps family members see and feel situations from each other's points of view, it also makes them realize that – when it comes down to it – they all love each other deeply and want what is best for each other. They are able to erase the assumption that family members are deliberately acting in hurtful ways, thus strengthening the relationship between them.

The Exchange exercise is also helpful for spouses whose partner "isn't a talker." Some people just don't communicate all that well verbally. If that's the case with your spouse, increasing empathy can help you best-guess what perspectives or emotions might be behind some of his or her behaviors.

To Do: Whenever your partner and/or another family member expresses a strong emotion – happiness or sadness, excitement or frustration, apathy or amusement – do your best to empathize with their feelings and situation. Make the effort to *feel* what they are feeling.

If you are struggling with a conflict in your marriage or family, schedule a time – one that is convenient for all family members – to perform The Exchange exercise. Remember that part one of the exercise, the "eyeball exchange," involves the effort to "see" a situation from another person's point of view. Part two of the exercise, the "emotion exchange," involves an effort to "feel" the situation from another person's point of view.

Be sure to create a casual, even enjoyable atmosphere in which to perform this exercise. Making it into more of a game than an exercise is a great idea, especially if you're involving young children. I often encourage family members to have fun with this exercise by wearing each other's clothes or shoes as they try to understand that person's perspective and emotions. This can bring humor and good spirits to the exercise, and prevent it from getting too serious. Yes, it's silly. And that's okay.

Day 21
Lifeline: Have an easygoing nature.

Sometimes it's okay to hold a grudge. In fact, there are times that it is actually warranted, especially when the offending party hasn't apologized or acknowledged what they've done, or there's a risk their behavior can harm you in some way.

But for the most part, holding a grudge against your spouse is a bad idea, especially when the offences are minor or unintended, as they so often are. When two people live together, day in and day out, a few missteps and annoyances are bound to happen.

How we as spouses react to these everyday missteps or annoyances has a profound effect on the overall quality of our marriage and can determine whether our marriage succeeds in the long-term.

A spouse who reacts with a critical spirit or who is quick to anger over small things – let's say a partner who loses the car keys or spills a quart of milk – will have his or partner and kids forever walking on eggshells in the home. Who wants to live like that?

In contrast, a spouse who lets small things slide, who reacts with good humor, humility and helpfulness, will create a happy, low-stress home where his or her partner and kids think the world of him or her.

Today's lifeline is about letting the "little things" slide and having an easygoing nature. Whether your partner is playing the music a little louder than you'd like, forgets to put the clothes in the dryer or burns supper, let it go.

Is it really that important in the big scheme of things?

Day 22
Lifeline: Respect.

I remember an occasion when my husband Don and I were rushing to get out of the house to make it to our son's parent-teacher interview on time. Don was trying to finish sending out a work email and I admit that my patience was wearing thin waiting for him. Finally, I gave him an exasperated sigh and went to wait in the car, closing the door just a little too hard behind me – you know, just for dramatic effect.

We hardly said a word to each other on the way to the school. When we arrived, our son's teacher was running late with the interviews and we had to sit in the hallway and wait for ten or fifteen minutes. When it was finally our turn, we sat down in front of the teacher. Despite the fact that she had made us wait, I was all smiles. I treated her with respect.

So why hadn't I managed to summon the same basic respect for my own husband when he was running late? Why the childish sighs and door slams? When you're married for a long time, like Don and I, you begin to take each other for granted. I've always had deep respect for Don as a person, husband and father, and I've never disrespected him in a "big" way. Yet there are times that I've found myself acting in ways that come across as disrespectful. Maybe I've rolled my eyes or used a tone of voice that I wouldn't have used on someone else.

Today's lifeline is about remembering to respect one's spouse. It is on remembering that our spouse isn't just our partner, he or she is a person that deserves our respect at all times. In fact, I can't think of a person who is more *deserving* of one's respect than his or her spouse. Who else has dedicated their life to you? Who else cares for you when you're ill and worries about you when you're down? Who else puts up with you, sticks by you, through thick and thin?

Extend this way of thinking to your interactions with other family members. There is a notion that children should inherently respect their parents; however, I don't agree with this. I think we as parents need to earn – not expect or demand – the respect of our children. The universe has entrusted them to our keeping for their most vulnerable years, and we need to have respect for that responsibility above all.

Indeed, I think it is impossible to demand respect from anyone, whether a spouse, child or employee. You may get what looks like respect back, but it isn't really respect at all – it's just obedience, and probably resentful obedience at that. Learn to recognize and appreciate the difference.

To Do: Whenever you look at your spouse, try to see him or her as a "person," just not your husband or wife. If you find yourself slipping into disrespectful behavior, ask yourself: "What gives me the right to treat or talk to this person with disrespect? Does this person deserve more from me?"

Also, ask yourself what you're doing to earn the respect of your children. Do they obey you because they respect you or because they fear you?

Day 23
Lifeline: Anticipate your partner's moods & needs.

When I'm meeting a client for the first time and trying to gauge the general state of his or her marriage, I will often test the waters by asking him or her a few questions such as, "What will your partner's mood be when he or she gets home after work tonight?" or "What would your partner like to do this weekend?"

Sometimes, the client will have fairly insightful answers. A husband might say, "Well, she had to chair a big meeting this morning at work, so I think she'll be drained when she gets home tonight" or "Well, there's a home show in town so I think she'd like to go do that on Saturday. I know she wants to redo our patio this summer."

Other times, the client is clueless. A husband might say, "How the hell should I know what kind of mood she'll be in?" or "I have no idea what she wants to do this weekend, I'm not a mind reader!"

What marriage do you think is standing on stronger legs?

We don't have to be mind-readers or psychics to have a good shot at predicting a spouse's mood, needs or preferences – not all the time, but some of the time.

The ability comes with knowing someone on a deeply intimate and familiar basis. It comes with sharing a life together, with knowing your spouse's schedule and caring enough to ask questions and stay plugged-in to what is going on in his or her life.

Spouses who are unable to predict a spouse's mood, needs or preferences have often stopped caring about what is going on in their partner's life.

They've stopped trying to make their partner happy. They've stopped trying to be helpful or supportive. They've lost the motivation to stay tuned-in to their spouse, marriage and home life. This kind of disconnect is a dangerous place to be, since it's often the first step toward the ultimate disconnect – divorce.

Today's lifeline strategy is about anticipating your partner's moods, needs and preferences.

The goal here isn't just to make your partner's life happier or easier, although that is a noble pursuit (and as a bonus, your partner is likely to return the favor by trying to make your life happier and easier).

The goal is also to "tune in" to your spouse, marriage and home life. It is to reconnect as true life partners. It is to avoid the kind of disconnect that just sneaks up on you, and that is the first silent step toward separation and divorce.

To Do: Today and every day, set aside a few minutes – morning, noon, after work and evening – to tune-in to your partner's life and anticipate his or her moods, needs and preferences.

Ask yourself: What is going on in my partner's life right now? What kind of mood might he or she be in today? If it's a sour one, how might I sweeten it? What could I do to make my partner's life happier, easier or less-stressed today or in the coming days?

Day 24

Lifeline: Challenge your assumptions.

Of all communication problems and misunderstandings a couple has, making assumptions – that is, jumping to conclusions – is definitely near the top of the list.

Even during the best of times, when we are thinking clearly and having positive feelings toward each other, it can be easy to make assumptions about what our partner might be doing, thinking or feeling.

When we are in conflict, however, the assumptions fall like acid rain. In the throes of emotion, anger and confusion, we fill in the blanks – Why is my partner late? What did my partner mean by that? Why did my partner do such a thing? – with the worst case scenario.

We assume a partner is late because he or she is having an affair or avoiding coming home. We assume a partner said a certain thing to be cruel or critical. We assume a partner acted a certain way because he or she wants to upset us or wants out of the marriage. Assumptions are almost always bad. And as often as not, they're wildly inaccurate, too.

One of the worst things about assumptions is that they lead a spouse to form a definite, negative opinion about his or her partner's actions, words or feelings.

This puts the "accused" partner in the unenviable position of having to defend himself or herself against the weight of this assumption.

None of us like being accused of things that we didn't do, think or feel. We might defend ourselves for a while – Of course I didn't do that! That isn't what I meant! That's not how I feel! – but at some point we're going to grow frustrated and indignant at our partner's assumptions and accusations, and the conflict is going to deepen.

Perhaps the saddest thing about assumptions is that they can mask truly positive intentions on the part of a spouse.

Take the case of a couple who has been bickering back and forth for a while. In an effort to make a loving gesture to his wife, the husband goes online to book his wife a surprise day at the spa. He looks through her daytimer to find out when her next day off is and schedules the appointment.

When the wife gets home, however, she notices that her daytimer is open. She immediately makes the assumption that her husband has been snooping through it, probably to see if she's been sharing lunch dates with a male co-worker.

She accuses her husband of this. Angry and hurt, he storms out the room. In his frustration, he makes his own assumption – why would she mention having lunch dates with a male co-worker unless she's been doing just that?

Today's lifeline is to challenge the negative assumptions you make about your partner's words, actions, feelings or intentions. Instead of jumping to conclusions, keep your feet on the ground. Use some patience and perspective.

Question your conclusions and check-your facts. If you're unsure about something your partner says or does, don't fill in the blanks with your own answers. Go straight to the source and ask your partner instead.

Day 25
Lifeline: Fight familiarity.

It is sometimes said that familiarity breeds contempt. I think that's often true. Or if not contempt, at least boredom and stagnation. And the last thing you want your marriage to become is boring and stagnant.

There is an artistic device known as defamiliarization. Most simply, this can be understood as the effort to present common, overly familiar things in a new and often expected way. The goal is to enhance our perception of what has become familiar to us, often so familiar that we don't notice it anymore. When we see something in a new and different light, we do a "double take." We notice it again. We even notice things about it that we never noticed before.

When two people have been married for a while, they become exceedingly familiar to each other. A wife can guess what shirt her husband is going to wear on a Monday morning, while he can guess what she's going to make for supper on Wednesday. They can predict each other's appearance, words, reactions, routines and behaviors.

To be sure, there is comfort and security in such predictability. It certainly isn't all bad. Yet there's a difference between being comfortable in a relationship and growing complacent in it. The first is loving and wonderful, but the latter is just plain lazy.

Today's lifeline strategy is to employ the technique of defamiliarization in your relationship. The challenge is to present yourself and your home in a new light, thus reinvigorating your marriage.

This can help you avoid or break-out of the "roommate rut" that so many couples fall into, where excessive familiarity has sapped the spice from their relationship so that they feel more like roomies or siblings than passionate life partners.

To Do: Take a look in the mirror. When was the last time you changed something about yourself? The style or color of the clothes you wear, your hairstyle, even your make-up or the fragrance you wear.

Remember that the point is to make your spouse do that "double take" when he or she looks at you, and to see you in a new way. New can be very appealing. Even a small change – wearing your hair differently, for example – can have a big effect.

In addition to defamiliarizing yourself, defamiliarize your space. Change something about your home – in particular your bedroom. Is it a sexy space? Does it have an erotic, enticing aura? If not, get to work. A married couple's bedroom should be a sensual sanctuary where they can retreat from the rest of the world and nourish their bond as husband and wife.

You can defamiliarization your routine and habits too, even with the smallest of things. Experiment with different foods or wine. If you typically watch romance movies, choose a horror flick instead. You get the idea.

Day 26
Lifeline: Sexual intimacy.

It sometimes happens that spouses get into a destructive (and completely pointless) debate about intimacy where they essentially pit emotional and sexual intimacy against each other. It's the old Love vs. Sex battle.

For example, a husband might say, "Why should I be more affectionate to my wife when she sexually rejects me?"

In response, the wife might say, "Why should I have sex with him when he doesn't show me any affection?" This kind of exchange is stereotypical, but it's one I've seen play out often in the office.

Emotional and sexual intimacy are two sides of the same coin. Within a marriage, they are equally important, even if each spouse seems to prefer or prioritize one of them.

Even when engaged in an argument like the above – where they seem polarized – both spouses will still admit that they want emotional and sexual intimacy within their marriage. They will agree that sex is an expression of love.

Marital love is made up of both emotional and sexual intimacy. Yet spouses' often different needs or preferences for each can make it seem like they are opposing rather than complementary forces.

There is a simple way to resolve this kind of conflict, and that is to remember that emotional intimacy must precede sexual intimacy within the context of a marriage.

Why? Because this approach is more likely to strengthen the relationship, thus leading to a good balance of emotional and sexual intimacy.

It is certainly a more respectful approach than pressuring a spouse to have sex when he or she is feeling a lack of emotional intimacy in the marriage.

It is certainly a more respectful approach than pouting when a spouse doesn't give in or withholding affection all the more, just to show a spouse how it feels to be rejected. Not only are these latter behaviors destructive, they are childish and incredibly off-putting.

Of course, sex is important. It's very important. In fact, regular access to sex with a trusted, loving partner is one of the main reasons people marry; however, marriage does not mean that a wife or husband is obligated to share her or his body, especially during those times that she or he feels a lack of emotional connection or warmth within the marriage.

If you find that sexual intimacy in your marriage is beginning to weaken, focus on what is going on outside the bedroom, not just inside it.

Are you and your spouse showing each other affection, appreciation and adoration? Is your marriage full of respect, fun and friendship? Emotional intimacy is the foundation upon which a great sex life is built.

This lifeline is about improving your sex life. Keep these five key points in mind as you strive to enhance sexual intimacy in your marriage:

1. Frequency. Many factors can impact sexual frequency, from exhaustion and lifestyle habits to natural aging and medical issues, and everything in between.

If you're not having sex as often as you used to – or as often as you'd like – work with your spouse to pinpoint the reason and problem-solve.

Whether it's visiting your doctor, getting in better shape or simply going to bed earlier, you and your spouse should work together to ensure that sex doesn't fall off the radar in your marriage.

2. **Variety.** Variety is the spice of life. It's the spice of sex, too. Sexual familiarity and routine – where you can predict all of your partner's twists and turns – is a real passion-slayer.

Focus on bringing variety and unexpected pleasures to sex. Brushing up on your sexual technique, trying new positions, reading erotica or experimenting with erotic aides is a good start. Being intimate at different times and in different places can help, too.

3. **Enthusiasm.** Good sexual skill and technique is important; however, sexual enthusiasm is just as important. Nobody likes a lazy or apathetic partner who just "lies there" or who looks like they're bored by lovemaking. We want to be with a partner who loses themselves in the pleasure and excitement of the experience. That kind of sexual enthusiasm is contagious and can bring a lot of energy to sex.

4. **Respect.** Sharing one's naked body in a sexually intimate way is a profoundly vulnerable experience. Spouses must take great care to respect each other's bodies, feelings and sensitivities during sex. As an extreme example of disrespect, I have seen cases where spouses will say, "You're getting too fat, I don't want to have sex with you anymore." Yes, serious weight gain can be problematic and needs to be managed; however, humiliating a sexual partner isn't just cruel, it is unacceptable.

5. **Mutual pleasure.** Selfish lovers are no fun. Not only is sexual selfishness a turn-off, it is also an immature and narcissistic quality that can quickly chip away at a couple's intimacy. When it comes to sex, both spouses should strive to put their partner's pleasure before their own. A spouse who feels like his or her pleasure is being prioritized is far more likely to prioritize his or her partner's pleasure.

Day 27

Lifeline: Humility.

We are living in what often appears to be an increasingly narcissistic society where people focus on and revere the "self" above all else.

Of course, there is such a thing as healthy self-love; however, that can be taken too far so that people extol their own virtues, opinions and needs above everyone else's – including those of their own spouse and children.

While narcissism is a complex psychological condition and there are many theories surrounding it, it can be informally understood as the excessive admiration and elevation of oneself.

As a behavior and concept, it originated with the Greek myth of Narcissus. Narcissus was a youth who fell in love with his own image as reflected in a pool of water. He was so focused on his own beauty that he gazed at himself until he died by the side of the water.

Without a doubt, narcissistic personality traits on the part of one or both spouses are the biggest barrier to a happy, healthy marriage and home life.

Why? Because people who exhibit narcissistic behaviors tend to make self-focused, often impulsive decisions without regard for the feelings of others, or for the consequences their behavior may have on others. They display a profound lack of empathy, concern or respect for other people in their life.

When it comes time to answer for their decisions, people with narcissistic tendencies become defensive, self-righteous and indignant. They avoid responsibility for their own actions or try to blame someone else for them.

They may even shrug off the worst of behaviors, from belligerence to chronic infidelity, with complete indifference. Instead of apologizing for their mistakes, they may display a sort of defiant pride by saying, "Well, that's just the way I am."

These behaviors make it impossible to move past problems or heal relationships.

Humility is the antidote to narcissistic traits. Humility is the ability to see one's behavior – especially one's negative behavior – clearly, and in the way that other people may see it. It is the ability to put our own behaviors and opinions in context.

Humility gives us the skill and grace to acknowledge our own negative behaviors, and to feel genuine regret for the effects those behaviors have had on the people we love.

Humility also gives us the ability to accept loving yet unflattering feedback from the people in our lives, so that we can take a self-critical look at our own behavior.

People who have humility are likely to enjoy the many benefits of long-term relationships in their lives.

People who lack humility are likely to end up divorced and estranged from family and friends.

Today's lifeline strategy is on bringing a spirit of respectful humility into your marriage and home life.

To do this, lead by example. Quickly and graciously acknowledge your shortcomings, and apologize when you say or do something unfair or insensitive. Give your spouse the sense that he or she is more important to you than your ego or pride.

Day 28
Lifeline: Learn to communicate.

In Shakespeare's masterpiece *Hamlet*, the dark prince is reading a book when he is asked by Polonius, a rather irritating old man, "What do you read, my lord?"

In reply, Hamlet says, "Words, words, words."

Looking for a more substantial answer, Polonius presses on to enquire about the subject matter of the book. He asks, "What is the matter, my lord?"

The prince responds, "Between who?"

Polonius won't give up. "I mean, the matter that you read, my lord."

You get where I'm going with this. Verbal communication is fraught with inherent problems and the potential for misunderstanding. In the play, Hamlet is being deliberately coy. He is steering the verbal misunderstanding with the skill of a captain steering a ship. The effect is amusing.

In real life, however, verbal misunderstandings are as unamusing – and unpredictable – as an unmanned ship lost at sea, being thrashed by the waves of a great storm. You never know where, when or even if it's going to crash against an unseen rocky shore. That is, you never know how your listener is going to interpret, or as likely misinterpret, what you say.

The problem with all those words, words, words is that we often put too much importance on them. We focus on the words our spouse says instead of the meaning and intent behind those words.

We focus on the words without trying to dig deeper and look for the motivating forces behind our spouse's words, including his or her emotions, expectations, hopes, fears, assumptions and self-perception.

There are many variables to communication. The words we use just scratch the surface.

When it comes to communication, word choice is just the tip of the iceberg. Couples who fail to recognize that fact are destined to have superficial argument after superficial argument without ever coming to a deeper understanding each other's position.

Today's lifeline is about listening less to the words your spouse uses and on hearing more of his or her actual message.

Listen to the message, not the words!

For example, take the case of an overworked wife. She gets home at the end of a long day to find that her husband didn't clear his breakfast dishes off the table. She says, "I'm so sick of being the maid around here! At least a maid gets paid for her work!"

At that, the husband says, "Nobody treats you like a maid. And you don't need to get paid, we have enough money for you to buy whatever you want."

Wow, talk about missing the point. Here, the husband has focused on the words "maid" and "paid." I suppose nobody can blame him. In this context they are incendiary words and the wife chose them for dramatic effect.

Yet because he focused on these loaded words, the husband didn't hear his wife's actual message: I'm stressed. I'm overworked. I feel unappreciated and unsupported. I'm tired and I feel like no one listens to me or takes my complaints seriously.

Here's another example. As the weekend nears, a husband says to his wife, "Can I have a few hours to play video games on Saturday night?"

At that, the wife says," You want to play video games? We have tons of home renovations to finish and we need to do a bunch of yard work. You know, grown up stuff. And we haven't had a date night in two months. But you want to play video games on Saturday night instead?"

Again, this spouse focused on the words "play video games" which, to her, sound like somewhat adolescent words to come out of a grown man's mouth. In so doing, she missed an important message from her husband: I'm exhausted. I really need a few hours to myself to wind down and do a fun, mindless activity.

When we focus only on words and our interpretation or misinterpretation of those words, we miss vital messages from those we love. We prevent essential information from travelling between spouses. Messages like "I'm stressed" or "I need a few hours to myself" are profoundly important to receive and respect.

But if words are just the tip of the iceberg when it comes to communicating, what is below the iceberg? Well, a lot of things. Emotions. Expectations. Assumptions. Fears. Unmet needs. Hopes. Intentions. Past issues. Self-perception. These are just a few of the messages we miss when we focus only on a partner's words.

To Do: Focus on "tuning out" your partner's words and "tuning in" to his or her message. If you find that you and your partner are misunderstanding each other, try to best-guess or speculate on your partner's message rather than just focusing on his or her "tip of the iceberg" words.

To help you do this, try to answer the following types of in-depth questions.

"Below the Iceberg" Questions:

What might my partner be feeling?

_____

_____

What might my partner be expecting?

_____

_____

What might my partner be assuming?

_____

_____

What might my partner be afraid of?

_____

_____

What might my partner be needing?

_____

_____

What might my partner be hoping?

_____

_____

What might my partner's true intention be?

_____

_____

What past issues – in my partner's life or in our marriage – might be on his or her mind?

_____

_____

What is my partner's self-perception?

_____

_____

These questions are not exhaustive; however, they do allow spouses to start digging a little deeper when it comes to communicating with each other, and to start realizing that mere words, words, words never tell the whole story.

Day 29
Lifeline: Manage intense emotion & anger.

We live in a society where people are increasingly hot-headed. Many have poor self-restraint and react with infantile outbursts or indignant outrage when things don't go their way.

Many have "hair triggers" that effectively hold family, friends and spouses as emotional hostages who must tiptoe around them for fear of setting off what is basically an adult temper tantrum and/or emotional meltdown.

People who display this kind of behavior aren't just immature, they are manipulative and controlling. They are also no fun to live with.

Whether it is a husband who "bullies" his wife to get his own way through anger or belligerence, or a wife who "guilt-trips" her husband to get her own way through tears or threats to leave, these folks need to grow up and get a grip on their behavior.

If you see these kinds of emotional outbursts in your marriage, this lifeline is for you. It might be your spouse who overreacts, it may be you, or it may be both of you.

Even if your marriage isn't burdened by emotional outbursts, this lifeline is still highly valuable for the insight it lends into your and your spouse's emotional reactions to various factors.

Today, the focus is on managing negative emotional outbursts.

Of course, the worst and most worrisome of these is anger; however, crying, threats of divorce, displays of belligerent defensiveness or criticism, and even withdrawing into total silence (or just failing to engage) are all forms of intense emotional overreactions that can cause harm in a marriage and that need to be managed.

To Do: Return to Part II and read the "A Belligerent, Critical or Defensive Spouse" heading. When you are finished, move on to complete the below exercise. While it is preferable for spouses to work together, you can work through this as a solo spouse. The goal is to gain insight into what causes negative behavioral outbursts and brainstorm ways to manage them.

As you work through this exercise, remember that good timing is important. Schedule a convenient time to work through or talk about this exercise. Create a mood of affection and open-mindedness. This exercise should be done in a positive spirit of discovery and healing.

As importantly, you must approach this exercise with a spirit of humility. It is absolutely essential that you and your spouse be willing to acknowledge your own inappropriate behavior. You can explain to your spouse why you react the way you do, but you cannot try to excuse, defend or justify it. While the interactions between you and your spouse may trigger your outbursts, in the end you are an adult and thus 100% accountable for your own overreactions.

Exercise: Managing emotional triggers & outbursts.

A. Reflect upon the arguments or conflicts that you and your spouse fall into. It may help to relive one or two arguments in your head so your memory and feelings are fresh.

List one to three emotions that trigger an outburst from you, whether that outburst is yelling, tears or withdrawal. That is, what feelings tend to trigger an emotional overreaction on your part?

(Note: Typical emotional triggers include: feeling unappreciated, unheard, insecure, fearful, disrespected, unsupported, unloved, unimportant, unnoticed, and so on.)

B. Reflect upon these arguments or conflicts from your partner's point of view.

Using your knowledge of your spouse, speculate on one to three emotions that trigger some kind of an outburst from him or her, whether that outburst is shouting, crying, falling silent or storming off.

Might your partner be feeling unappreciated, unheard, disrespected, fearful or unloved when he or she reacts with this kind of intense emotion?

If you are working through this exercise with your spouse, you can share your speculative answers about each other. The goal is to put empathetic effort into understanding your partner's emotional triggers and then to ensure that your understanding is accurate.

C. Brainstorm ways to reduce the frequency and severity of the emotional overreactions in your relationship.

Once you and your spouse have an understanding of your respective emotional triggers, you can work together to manage each other's triggers and ensure that peace reigns supreme in your marriage.

This can be done in any number of ways. Some couples may have to make lifestyle changes or implement new relationship rules. Others may wish to use a visual or verbal cue to "notify" a partner that he or she has started to overreact.

Yet quite often, it is enough to simply be aware of what emotions trigger an overreaction in our spouse. If we know our partner is triggered by a feeling of disrespect, we strive to speak to him or her with a more respectful voice tone. We remember to say "please" and "thank you," and we call or text if we're going to be unexpectedly late.

The best way to manage outbursts is to have the type of relationship dynamics that make them unnecessary.

Let's look at an example that will bring this exercise to life. Consider the case of a wife who "freaks out" when her husband goes away for a golf weekend. Normally, he resents her and thinks she is trying to control him. He accuses her of that, and the fight is on.

Upon reflection, however, he suspects that her outbursts are triggered not by a controlling nature, but instead by feelings of being unappreciated. After all, she has to stay home with two small kids while he goes to have fun. And she hasn't had a break in a while.

To manage this emotional trigger, he tells her how much he appreciates her sacrifice to stay home with the kids so that he can enjoy his golf weekend, and how much he knows she needs a break, too. He acknowledges the impact his golf weekend has on her life.

He tells her that he is treating her to a spa day when he gets back to show his appreciation for all that she does, and that he will give her a much-needed break from the kids.

It is now more likely that his wife feels appreciated for her sacrifices, and that she will support his golf getaway.

Instead of competing for what they each want, this couple competes in the other direction – to make their partner happy.

Day 30
Lifeline: Resolve conflict.

Many of the lifelines in *Marriage SOS* are designed to help couples avoid conflict; however, conflict will always happen, even in the happiest and most stable of relationships.

Whether it's occasional bickering over housework or an angry blow-up over an unpleasant situation, couples are bound to argue and face conflict.

The important part is that they get past it, and that they do so in a way that strengthens the marriage, not weakens it.

Today's lifeline is one that will take some time. It focuses on resolving conflict in a positive and purposeful way, and it requires that you draw upon several strategies from past days. Therefore, I will ask you to refresh your memory by quickly reviewing the below lifelines.

Day 1 (voice tone); Day 5 (get to the root of arguments); Day 7 (take a detour); Day 14 (face your fears); Day 18 (your spouse's unmet needs); Day 20 (empathy); Day 21 (have an easygoing nature); Day 24 (challenge your assumptions); Day 28 (learn to communicate) and; Day 29 (manage intense emotion & anger).

Reinforcing these lifelines can help you move past many types of conflict; however, there are some issues that will require a specific problem-solving strategy if you are to resolve them once and for all.

For example, conflict surrounding spending, parenting decisions, schedules and chores all require real-world solutions if they are to stop wreaking havoc in the home.

This requires that couples have a problem-solving strategy or method that they can fall back on when an issue needs to be hammered out and workable solutions need to be found.

A "Pros & Cons" List

Sometimes, a simple list of "pros and cons" can help people arrive at a workable solution to a problem. Keep in mind, however, that each spouse and family member may have their own subjective list of pros and cons. As long as that is taken into consideration, a list of pros and cons is an easy but effective way to decide on the best course of action for a given problem.

The act of putting pen to paper as you brainstorm ways to resolve problems is a remarkably effective way to end pointless, ongoing verbal speculations or arguments. When we are forced to focus and write down potential solutions to a problem, we tend to argue less and collaborate more.

A "Problem-Solving" Flowchart

Creating a problem-solving flowchart is another way that couples can put pen to paper and stay focused long enough to brainstorm potential solutions to a specific problem. Below is a very simple problem-solving flowchart. Use it as a simple guide to work through your problems, or amend it to your preferences.

The value of such flowcharts isn't in some kind of elaborate design. It is on their ability to help couples stay on-track and maintain a forward momentum during the process of working through an issue. And isn't that half the battle?

We all know how easy it is to start spinning our wheels when we're trying to figure out a problem, especially a complicated problem that involves unknown or numerous factors, competing preferences or challenging schedules. If you can avoid spinning your wheels, you're on the road to resolving the issue.

Following the map of a problem-solving flowchart brings structure to a chaotic, emotional and confusing process. Best of all, it takes the needs and interests of both spouses into account, so that solutions work for both of them.

A 7-Step Problem-Solving
Flowchart for Couples and Families

1. Identify the problem (i.e. excessive debt).

2. Gather facts relevant to the problem (i.e. income, expenses, lifestyle, etc.).

3. Brainstorm potential solutions to the problem based on the facts you have gathered (i.e. make a new budget, get a different job, move into a less expensive home, postpone a vacation, give control of the finances to one spouse, etc.).

Assessing the suitability of a potential solution may require further fact-finding or consideration (i.e. checking the state of the job market, finding out the value of current home, seeing whether you can receive a refund from booked airline tickets, asking whether a spouse has time to take control of the finances, etc.).

4. Ask how each potential solution will impact each partner and/or family member. Remember that solutions have to work for each person in the home.

5. Create an action plan. Choose what appears to be the best solution based on the facts and its impact on each family member.

6. Implement the action plan. Decide when the action plan will begin and how long it will last, if that is relevant (i.e. one spouse will control the finances for six months). Discuss any details that need to be worked out for the plan to function (i.e. how will the spouse who has control of the money allocate spending money to the family?).

7. Observe results. Determine when or how often (i.e. weekly or monthly) you will review the action plan to see whether it is working and whether everyone in the home is reasonably satisfied with it.

If the action plan is not resolving the problem, begin the process over by starting with step 1 of this flowchart.

SUPPLEMENT

Articles

Over the years, I have contributed to many media outlets in Canada, the United States and worldwide. In the following pages, I have presented a handful of marriage-minded articles I've written for THE HUFFINGTON POST. These are articles that I received quite a bit of positive feedback on from readers, so I thought I'd include them here as a little supplemental reading.

I hope you will find a few gems of insight or information within these articles that will reinforce the content in this book. At the very least, they are good reminders that offer quick ideas to get you in a pro-marriage mindset.

Stop Talking Your Relationship to Death!

Many of us have been in a work meeting that went on for WAAAAY too long. The same people, saying the same things, over and over again. The same people complaining ad nauseam, using the meeting structure as an opportunity to vent about everything that is wrong with the company, its policies or their co-workers.

And they don't just state their complaint once and move on. Oh no. They state their complaint several times, often launching into long, drawn-out anecdotes to illustrate in excruciating detail just how bad things are.

With every anecdote, the situation becomes even more dire and hopeless. *Truly, this is the worst company ever! It's days away from bankruptcy! We're doomed! There's no way things can get better...I've been thinking of looking for a new job! Yes, it's that bad!*

And then, just when some exasperated soul suggests moving on to solutions, everyone looks at the clock. "Oh, it's lunch. Let's regroup at this time tomorrow."

The only things that are accomplished in a meeting like this -- which is all talk and no action -- are a sense of futility, deep irritation and a growing dislike of our co-workers. The longer it goes on, the less you care about solving problems or improving the workplace. All you care about is getting the hell out of that shrinking, stuffy boardroom and taking a breath of fresh air outside.

Now imagine this scenario involves a husband and wife in a marriage counsellor's office.

While counselling and talk therapy can work wonders for some people, other people who are struggling with marriage issues find them to be ineffective or, worse, damaging. Too few counsellors focus on moving forward toward practical, real-world strategies for couples who are in crisis.

Instead, some spouses attend weekly visits where they talk about their problems for an hour, digging up the proverbial dead cat and then burying it again until the following week. Sessions are often filled with anger, finger-pointing and tears, and couples often fight in the car on the ride home. All of this makes it impossible for a couple to feel that they will ever be able to bury their problems once and for all.

Infidelity is a classic case. It's one of the most painful experiences a couple can undergo, and it is absolutely essential that spouses begin to take actual steps toward recovery instead of just talking about it. In fact, this "actions speak louder than words" is the entire platform of my book COUPLES IN CRISIS: OVERCOMING INFIDELITY & OPPOSITE-SEX FRIENDSHIPS.

Yet it isn't just big problems like infidelity that require actions alongside (fewer) words. Even smaller issues can swell into major ones if we talk about them too much.

So what's my suggestion? Well, it's impossible to offer a one-size-fits-all solution here. What I can suggest, however, is that you honestly reflect upon how often you talk (and talk and talk) about your problems. Is your approach working?

If not, bite your tongue. Instead, let your actions speak for you. Focus on improving the quality of your interactions with your spouse.

Offer to pour him a cup of morning coffee. Bring her flowers. Watch a favourite film together. Express your appreciation for everything your spouse does, and praise him or her in front of your children. Share chores. Try to make your spouse's life easier every day.

When your spouse walks by, offer him or her a warm smile. Prioritize your emotional and sexual intimacy. Have transparency in your marriage in terms of passwords and access to technology. Put your smartphones in the desk drawer when you get home and connect with your spouse instead of texting your friend.

And when you do talk, be sure to remove tones of criticism, contempt and defensiveness in your voice and replace them with tones of affection, humility and friendship.

Of course, some relationship problems do have to be discussed. But trust me -- *if you improve your interactions before you talk about them*, you'll spend a lot less time digging up and re-burying cats that should have been laid to rest a long time ago.

Plus, many people already know their partner's complaints. They already know what their marriage problems are. With a little bit of thought, they can figure out what changes in their behaviour might help improve things. Talking about it (again!) isn't really necessary.

If that resonates with you, challenge yourself to act first and talk second. You might be surprised how many problems can be resolved without saying a single word.

* * * * * * * * * *

8 Tips to Affair-Proof Your Marriage

1. **Don't ignore your partner's complaints.** It is foolish, short-sighted and selfish to shrug off a partner's complaints, whether they are about housework, money, a lack of affection, in-laws or texting. It is even worse to become ignorant or defensive when your partner tries to express the reasons for his or her unhappiness. You don't need to agree with what he or she is saying. But you do need to listen, care and do something to improve the situation.

2. **Don't let sex fall off the radar.** Sex is a big part of marriage. In fact, regular sexual intimacy is a prevailing reason to get married. Order-in supper more often, put the kids to bed earlier, chew on a handful of chocolate-covered coffee beans before bed -- do whatever it takes to keep some energy for sex. If you are having relationship problems that are standing in the way of a healthy sex life, fix them. Get professional help if you must. But stop making excuses.

3. **Show interest in your partner's life.** Ask yourself every day, "What can I do to make my partner's life happier and easier?" If both partners are doing this, you have it made.

4. **Have fun together.** When was the last time you and your partner shared a good belly laugh? When was the last time you couldn't stop smiling? If it's been a while, you need to "lighten up" your relationship. People are naturally drawn toward those who are fun to be around.

5. **Appreciate your partner.** Not a day should go by that you don't express appreciation for your partner in words and deed. Feeling

unappreciated is a major complaint in almost all troubled marriages.

6. **Put technology in its place.** Translation: *Put down the damn phone and talk to your partner!* Nothing is more irritating than feeling second-place to a smartphone.

7. **Talk to your partner like he or she is someone you love.** Be vigilant of your voice tone and manners. Keep contempt, defensiveness, criticism and rudeness out of your marriage.

8. **Create shared rituals.** Whether it's binge-watching *The Walking Dead* on Sunday nights or Sunday night walks in the park, it is important for couples to have traditions. These give couples a sense of identity and continuity as a couple.

* * * * * * * * *

Be Honest: Do You Throw "Texting Tantrums"?

My husband Don and I were out for dinner the other night when, at the table next to us, a three-year-old boy launched into a classic temper tantrum. After being denied his third glass of soda -- an injustice of epic proportions when you still use a sippy cup -- he proceeded to throw his food at his mother, kick his dad under the table with all his might and scream, "I hate you!" at the top of his lungs. It was quite the show.

Scenes like this are never flattering to the players. They're even less flattering when the players are old enough to know better. I mean, you'd assume that a person who has to use the fingers on both hands to show his age would have left these infantile outbursts of self-indulgent anger behind him, right? Wrong.

The adult temper tantrum is alive and well. Although it takes many unpleasant forms, one of the most common is what I call a "texting tantrum."

Not a week goes by that I don't have a client hold up a cell phone and say, "Look at what my partner has been saying to me!" The text-fight between them is always the same: Name calling; Profanity; Insults; Upper case letters meant to convey JUST HOW F*&^CKING STUPID the other person is; One. Word. Sentences. With. Periods. To. Really. Emphasize. Just. How. Done. I. Am. With. Your. B@llsh*t.

I've seen text-fights that lasted for hours and involved literally hundreds of back-and-forth digital missives, each more contemptuous than the last. The anger, misinterpretation and vitriol in text-fights escalate with the speed and force of a runaway train filled with explosives.

Unlike a face-to-face argument, there are no safety checks to slow down a text-fight. There's no opportunity to shake your head and say, "Wait, that's not what I meant! I love you, let's bring this down a notch." There's no chance to defuse the situation with a spark of affection or humour, a soft word or even an unexpected embrace. There's only unbridled, unchecked, unrestrained and utterly self-focused emotion and assumption.

So what's the solution? Well, that's easy. Stop texting. OMG, right?! Well, get a grip on yourself. Texting is not your only communication option. And it certainly isn't an essential way to communicate. Is it convenient? Yes, at times it can be. But the moment texting becomes a source of conflict rather than convenience, it's time to delete this form of communication from your relationship.

How long should you refrain from texting? A month? Six months? There's no magic number. I suppose my answer would be, "Until you have moved past your relationship problems, can demonstrate more respect for your partner, and can show an adult-level of self-restraint."

If you twist my arm and demand a number -- which I know you want to do -- I'd say that couples who regularly fall into these kinds of extreme text-fights should stop texting altogether for a period of three months at an absolute minimum, during which time they must tackle the deeper relationship issues that exist. Happy, healthy couples simply don't speak to each other this way.

After this time, those couples who wish to reintroduce texting into their communication must first lay a few ground rules.

Text messages must always begin with a greeting such as, "Hi sweetheart" or even a simple "Hello." For those people who are prone to text-fights, it is important to start a message off with a polite greeting. Launching into a text message without a brief greeting is like storming into a room and talking before you've said hello. It can come across as abrupt, invasive, self-important and demanding.

If a partner does not respond, do not text him or her again. It is irritating to pick up one's phone only to find twenty messages saying, "Where are you?" and "Why aren't you answering me!" and "Call me NOW!" Almost always, this kind of pattern snowballs into typical text-fight frustration, hostility and accusation.

A text message must serve at least one of three purposes. It must either: a) convey a positive emotional message; b) convey information in a respectful and thorough way, and/or; c) serve as a positive way to stay connected during the day via brief "I love you"s, "xoxo"s or happy-sweet emoticons or symbols.

Finally, text messages must always end with a loving and clear sign-off. When does a text message conversation end? Even between friends or happy spouses, it can sometimes be unclear. To avoid a spouse mistakenly believing that his or her partner has just stopped responding, couples must always make it clear that the texting conversation is over.

A spouse might text, "OK, I'm going to get back to work now...anything else before I go?" If the other partner responds "No," then the spouse can end the conversation with a respectful, "Love you, chat later." This lets a partner know that his or her texts won't be responded to for a while. It might even be a good idea to let a partner know when you might next be looking at your phone. Texting a brief, "Will check my phone at lunch time" can prevent all kinds of confusion, unnecessary speculation and escalating irritation.

Even for those couples who are not prone to text-fights, following these texting ground rules can go a long way toward avoiding pointless arguments and assumptions. Texting is the demon child of the communication world, and the more you can prevent an innocent text from being misinterpreted -- and potentially spiraling into a texting tantrum -- the better.

* * * * * * * * * *

Why Opposite-Sex Friendships Will Destroy Your Marriage

While there are a lot of ways to screw up a marriage, spouses who have close opposite-sex friendships are toying with one of the riskiest and most short-sighted behaviours that commonly lead to infidelity and ultimately divorce.

Many of my consults begin with a client saying something like this: *"My husband is constantly texting a female co-worker...he says they're just friends and that they only talk about work, but he's always laughing and smiling when he's texting her."*

Or this: *"I know my wife is always texting or on Facebook with her personal trailer. Now she locks her cell phone and has changed her online passwords. If I ask her who she's talking to, she freaks out and says I'm being paranoid, jealous and controlling."*

Do you know what the above scenarios have in common? In both of them, the spouse who is having the opposite-sex friendship knows full-well that the behaviour is as shady as hell. But instead of respecting their spouse's feelings, they continue to indulge in the ego-boost or thrill of it all.

Some people don't agree with my stance that opposite-sex friendships should not exist within marriage. Some people might say that it is old-fashioned and that men and women are perfectly capable of having platonic extra-marital friendships with a person of the opposite sex.

In cases where the friendship involves two people who have absolutely no sexual attraction to each other and who are not sexually compatible whatsoever, that is very true.

But in reality, many opposite-sex friendships involve people who - if circumstances were different - might be potential sexual partners. Indeed, many opposite-sex friendships are maintained because of a simmering attraction. One or both people are keeping their "friend" on the back-burner as a potential mate in the event their current relationship ends.

This is especially true of men. Let's face it, many men still only befriend women they have at least some degree of physical attraction to.

Some people will say that they've always had opposite-sex friendships and that shouldn't change just because they get married. They will say that only insecure people or weak marriages would shy away from opposite-sex friendships.

In my opinion, this is a self-focused and naïve way of thinking. It ignores the reality that every marriage goes through ups and downs. When you're "up," things are great and the opposite-sex friendship may be mostly harmless (although it still may be an irritation to the other spouse).

But it's a different story when you're going through a temporary "down" or rough patch in your relationship. This might be some kind of conflict, sexual dry spell, life circumstance or even pure boredom. When this happens, many people turn to their opposite-sex friend as a shoulder to cry on.

Before you know it, the spouse and his or her extra-marital friend are comforting each other, turning to each other for advice, sharing details of their intimate life and relationships, and texting each other with increasing frequency and intimacy. As the excitement of their forbidden friendship grows, the dynamics in the marriage deteriorate. After all, three's a crowd.

The spouse begins to leave the room to text his or her opposite-sex friend, leaving the other spouse in a state of anger, anxiety and profound hurt.

When asked to end the friendship, the spouse often becomes indignant or outright belligerent, and may try to turn the entire situation around so that his or her spouse must go on the defensive, desperately trying to explain -- to no avail -- why the opposite-sex friendship is wrong and how it is affecting the marriage.

In my capacity as a couples mediator, I can tell you that the vast majority of infidelities I see nowadays follow a similar pattern to this one.

They start with an opposite-sex friendship that quickly becomes intense and emotional due to the false sense of intimacy involved with text-messaging. They then escalate into a full-blown emotional or sexual affair.

Not only are opposite-sex friendships within marriage risky, they are a form of betrayal. When a person gets married or enters into an exclusive committed relationship, that person expects to be his or her partner's lover, closest and most intimate confidante, and priority. Of course, we all need close friendships outside of our marriage; however, there are plenty of people of our own gender to befriend.

Opposite-sex friendships can also sneak-up on people in otherwise happy relationships, particularly when the opposite-sex friend is a "partner predator."

This kind of opposite-sex friend may come across as innocent, but is drawn to someone who is already "taken" and can be very manipulative and aggressive in their pursuit of this person. If they manage to befriend your spouse, get ready for a world of trouble and drama.

In my opinion, it's simply foolish to disregard the strong association between opposite-sex friendships in marriage and infidelity. Deciding that these have no place in your marriage is one of the wisest and most pro-active measures you can take to protect the integrity of your relationship in the long-term.

It isn't weak or insecure to do this. It takes a strong person to stand by their values and to insist that there be no opposite-sex friendships within marriage.

It takes a secure person to say, "I'm not living like this. I won't live with the uncertainty and the anxiety and the divided loyalties. I won't pretend that I'm not hurt because you're putting energy into this friendship instead of our relationship." Stand by your values and vision of marriage -- you know, that whole "forsaking all others" business -- and trust your instincts.

* * * * * * * * * *

8 Ways to Take Your Marriage Off "Hold"

Most of us have heard of the so-called child-centered marriage. It's where a couple focuses most of their time, energy and affection on their children and very little on each other. Of course, those of us who have kids at home know that the little darlings are demanding creatures (it's why Mother Nature made them so cute) and prioritizing our relationship is often easier said than done. After all, the squeaky wheel gets the oil. And kids are usually squeakier than adults (well, at least they should be).

I've worked with too many couples who -- once that nest is empty -- find that they have neglected their relationship for so long that their partnership and passion for each other have seriously waned. That's a sad thing. It's heartbreaking to see a couple who has devoted so much time and emotion to raising great kids then face divorce at a time when they should be enjoying their newfound freedom.

It's a mistake to think that you can put your relationship "on hold" until the kids are gone. Instead, practice these eight ways to take your marriage "off hold" right now, and keep it alive and well throughout the various stages of your life together.

1. Indulge your adult tastes. Many parents fall into the rut where every movie and meal revolves around their kids' preferences. Some parents even feel guilty when they want to watch or eat something their kids don't like. Trust me: it's fine to leave the kids with a sitter so you can catch an R-rated movie or dine at a restaurant that doesn't have a clown painted on the walls.

2. Romance your partner. Whether it's flowers, spontaneous embraces, flirtatious winks or admiring looks, make sure your partner knows that you desire him or her and that the spark is still there. Model for your kids what a loving, long-term romantic partnership looks like.

3. Fan the flames of passion. Make sure that you're saving enough time and energy for regular sexual intimacy. Focus on your partner's pleasure as well as your own, and try to bring variety into the bedroom. If you're the partner who always initiates, ask your spouse what you can do (or stop doing!) to spark his or her interest. If you rarely or never initiate, take the lead and do so. It means more than you think.

4. Respect your partner as a person. Your spouse isn't just a husband or wife, father or mother. Your spouse is a unique individual. Help your spouse find time to pursue his or her interests, socialize with friends or have alone time (and don't guilt-trip him or her for doing so).

5. Nourish your partnership. Marriage and family life take teamwork. Work together in all things from housework to financial planning. Parent as a united front, keeping disagreements behind closed doors. Show appreciation for your partner and praise him or her in front of your kids. If your partner has a complaint about your relationship, listen with an open mind and an open heart. At the same time, be sure to express your own complaints with respect, love and humility.

6. Put technology in its place. Put your smartphone in a drawer when you get home and make sure Facebook doesn't replace face-to-face conversation. Nothing is more annoying (or hurtful) than being ignored by partner who is forever texting, posting or updating something or other. Unplug and reconnect with those who matter.

7. Stay attractive to your partner. Eating well, staying reasonably fit and dressing nicely doesn't just keep us looking good for our partner, it keeps us feeling good about ourselves.

Yet attraction goes beyond appearance. It's about behaviour, too. A spouse who is easygoing, supportive and good-natured is more attractive than one who is short-tempered, self-centered or negative. It also doesn't hurt to have interesting things to talk about, rather than always discussing the kids, work or bills.

8. Past, present and future. Revisit old pics to remember the good times and put down roots. A sense of shared history is important. At the same time, live in the moment and realize that this amazing time in your life -- this time when you and your children all live under the same roof -- will pass faster than you think. Finally, have a shared vision of your future together: it will remind you that life and marriage go on even after the kids have moved on.

A Final Word to Readers

Despite the "hard line" I often take with couples and the many struggling marriages I have seen up close and personal over the years, I am still a hopeless romantic. I believe that two people can stay married for life and that their lives are far richer for it.

You've chosen this book because your relationship is struggling, and I sincerely hope that you have found strategies herein that will help you improve your marriage and home life. Spouses can overcome all manner of marriage problems. They can even enjoy healthier and happier marriages because they have overcome those problems. That happens every single day, and it can happen for you, too.

We don't always learn about each other or ourselves when the skies are blue. Sometimes, we need to weather a storm or two before we learn how to keep our marriages afloat. We need to work together to rescue our relationship so that we can sail off into the sunset together. This sentiment isn't an empty or cliché one. It is a realistic one. And it is the guiding force behind Marriage SOS.

I wish you and your family all the best.

Debra Macleod, B.A., LL.B.,
Couples Mediator & Author-Expert

ABOUT THE AUTHOR

Debra Macleod, B.A., LL.B., is a top-tier couples mediator, marriage author and expert resource for major media, from THE NEW YORK TIMES to ELLE Magazine. Her private practice, Marriage SOS, helps couples avoid divorce and improve their marriages and home lives.

Look for Debra's other books in the Marriage SOS book series:

Couples In Crisis: Overcoming Affairs & Opposite-Sex Friendships: A Fast & Innovative Approach to Rebuild Trust and Revive Your Marriage (Not Talk It To Death)

Marriage SOS: Blended Family Edition

Marriage SOS: Oilpatch Edition

Visit Debra's website at MarriageSOS.com

13463524R00105

Made in the USA
Lexington, KY
31 October 2018